THE XXL AIR FRYER COOKBOOK UK

Easy, Affordable & Super-Delicious Air Fryer Recipes For Friends & Family I All Time Favorite Recipe Collection I Poultry, Meat, Vegetarian, Vegan, Snacks & More

AMANDA GREENE

TABLE OF CONTENTS

EXCLUSIVE BONUS

40 Weight Loss Recipes

&

14 Days Meal Plan

Scan the QR-Code and receive
the FREE download:

Introduction

1. The Air Fryer Landscape

The kitchen appliance world is continually evolving, with innovations designed to make cooking easier, healthier, and more enjoyable. Among these innovations, air fryers have captured the attention of cooking enthusiasts and health-conscious individuals alike, not just in the United Kingdom but around the globe. Their surge in popularity has led to an array of models flooding the market, each with unique features tailored to different cooking styles and needs.

The principle behind air frying is astonishingly simple but exceptionally effective. By circulating hot air around the food, the air fryer creates a crispy exterior similar to that of traditionally fried foods but without the need for submerging the items in oil. This allows for a healthier, less greasy, but equally delicious end product. Whether you're looking to whip up a quick snack or prepare a more elaborate dish, the air fryer's versatility can accommodate a wide array of recipes, which this cookbook will introduce you to.

As with any tool, understanding the landscape of available options, capabilities, and even limitations is essential for making the most out of it. This section has laid the groundwork by offering an overview of what an air fryer is and how it fits into the broader context of culinary innovation. Subsequent sections will delve deeper into other essential topics, helping you master the art of air frying.

2. Air Frying for Health and Wellness

For many people, the primary draw of air frying is its health benefits. Traditional frying methods often require a substantial amount of oil, contributing to a higher fat and calorie content in the finished dish. Air fryers, however, use a fraction of the oil, drastically reducing the fat content and calories without sacrificing the crunch or flavour that we all love in fried foods.

The appeal of this cooking method goes beyond merely reducing the fat content. Air frying also retains more nutrients in your food compared to methods like boiling or grilling. And because air frying is so quick and efficient, it's an excellent option for those with busy lifestyles who are keen to maintain a balanced diet. Meals that once required an hour in the oven can often be prepared in half the time, making it easier than ever to incorporate homemade, nutritious foods into your daily routine.

Furthermore, the air fryer isn't just for those who eat meat. Vegetarians and vegans will find this appliance incredibly useful for preparing a wide array of plant-based dishes, all without the need for excessive oils or fats. From crispy tofu to succulent vegetable medleys, the air fryer can do it all, and usually in less time than traditional methods.

In summary, the air fryer offers a versatile, time-efficient, and healthier alternative to traditional cooking methods. Whether you're someone who's counting calories, watching nutrient intake, or simply looking to make healthier choices, the air fryer has a significant role to play in your journey towards health and wellness.

3. Navigating Your Air Fryer Settings

Understanding the settings on your air fryer is crucial for optimising your cooking experience. While most air fryers are relatively user-friendly, each model may have unique features that set it apart from others. This chapter aims to provide a general overview to help you navigate your way through the array of settings and options you might encounter.

Temperature Control:

One of the first settings you'll notice is the temperature control, often ranging from around 80 degrees Celsius to 200 degrees Celsius. The correct temperature setting depends on what you're cooking—lower temperatures are typically suitable for delicate items like fish, while higher settings are best for achieving a crispy finish on items like chips or chicken wings.

Time Settings:

Most air fryers also feature a timer, which usually goes up to 30 or 60 minutes. The time you set will again depend on what you're cooking. Some recipes might require you to shake the basket or flip the food halfway through, so keep an eye on the timer.

Preheat Function:

Some models come with a preheat function, which brings the air fryer to the desired temperature before you insert your food. This can ensure a more even cook and is particularly useful for items that require high heat right from the start.

Special Modes:

Many modern air fryers come with preset modes for commonly cooked items like chips, poultry, or vegetables. While these can be handy, remember that they are generalized settings and might not be perfectly calibrated for your specific recipe. It's always a good idea to check your food for doneness before the timer runs out.

Safety Features:

Some air fryers offer additional safety features like automatic shut-off or a lock function to prevent accidental changes to the settings. While these may not directly relate to the cooking process, they can provide peace of mind, especially if you have young children.

By familiarising yourself with these fundamental settings, you'll be better equipped to use your air fryer to its full potential. Once you get the hang of it, you'll find that the air fryer is not just a healthier cooking alternative but also an incredibly versatile addition to your kitchen arsenal.

4. Safety First: Air Fryer Usage Guidelines

While air fryers are designed with safety in mind, it's crucial to be aware of the do's and don'ts to ensure a hazard-free cooking experience. This chapter will delve into some of the key safety measures you should consider when using your air fryer.

Placement of the Air Fryer:

Your air fryer should be placed on a flat, stable surface with plenty of room for ventilation. Keep it away from walls or other appliances to ensure proper airflow, as this can be essential for its performance and longevity.

Electrical Safety:

Make sure that your electrical outlet is compatible with the air fryer's voltage requirements. Avoid using an extension cord if possible, and always ensure the air fryer is unplugged when not in use.

Handling the Basket:

The air fryer basket will be hot during and after cooking, so always use oven mitts or heat-resistant gloves when removing it. Also, never shake the basket without first pausing the air fryer.

Overloading:

To ensure even cooking, do not overload the air fryer basket. Overcrowding can lead to unevenly cooked food and may even cause the appliance to malfunction due to restricted airflow.

Use of Oil:

Air fryers require significantly less oil than traditional frying methods, but if your recipe does call for oil, make sure to use it sparingly. Always add oil to the food and not directly into the air fryer basket unless specifically instructed by the manufacturer.

Cleaning and Maintenance:

It's essential to keep your air fryer clean to maintain its performance and safety. Ensure all parts are cool to the touch before attempting any cleaning. The basket and tray are often dishwasher-safe, but always consult the manufacturer's instructions for proper care.

Supervision:

Never leave your air fryer unattended while in use, especially if children or pets are around. Most models have safety features like automatic shut-off, but it's best to stay nearby to monitor its operation.

By adhering to these safety guidelines, you're not just protecting yourself but also ensuring that your air fryer remains a reliable and efficient tool in your cooking ventures. Remember, the better you treat your appliance, the longer it will last and the better it will perform.

EXCLUSIVE BONUS

40 Weight Loss Recipes

&

14 Days Meal Plan

Scan the QR-Code and receive
the FREE download:

Chapter 1:
Breakfast and Brunch Favourites (20 recipes)

BLACK PUDDING HASH BROWNS

Servings: 4 | Difficulty: Medium | Temperature: 200 degrees Celsius | Preparation Time: 15 minutes | Cooking Time: 20 minutes

INGREDIENTS:

- ✪ 400g black pudding
- ✪ 400g potatoes
- ✪ 1 white onion
- ✪ 1 tablespoon olive oil
- ✪ 1/2 teaspoon salt
- ✪ 1/4 teaspoon ground black pepper
- ✪ fresh parsley for garnish

PREPARATION:

1. Peel and grate the potatoes and onion.
2. In a dry tea towel, squeeze out any excess moisture from the grated potatoes and onion.
3. In a large bowl, crumble the black pudding, add the grated potatoes, onion, olive oil, salt, and ground black pepper. Mix until the ingredients are well combined.
4. Form the mixture into the shape of hash browns and place them in a single layer in your air fryer basket.
5. Cook the hash browns in your preheated air fryer at 200 degrees Celsius for 15-20 minutes. Flip them over halfway through so they cook evenly. The hash browns should be crispy on the outside and cooked through on the inside.
6. Once cooked, sprinkle with a little bit more salt if desired, garnish with fresh parsley and serve your Black Pudding Hash Browns hot. It's a hearty and crisp treat to please any appetite.

NUTRITION FACTS PER 100G:
Energy: 210kcal | Protein: 8.3g | Total Fat: 13.4g | Saturated Fat: 5.1g | Carbohydrates: 14.1g | Sugars: 0.3g | Dietary Fibre: 0.9g

FULL ENGLISH BREAKFAST TRAY

Servings: 2 | Difficulty: Medium | Temperature: 200 degrees Celsius |
Preparation Time: 10 minutes | Cooking Time: 20 minutes

INGREDIENTS:

- 4 British-style sausages
- 200g button mushrooms
- 2 ripe tomatoes, halved
- 4 rashers of back bacon
- 2 large free-range eggs
- 400g tinned baked beans
- 2 thick slices of black pudding
- salt and pepper to taste
- 1 tablespoon sunflower oil

PREPARATION:

1. Preheat the air fryer to 200 degrees Celsius.
2. Brush the fryer basket lightly with sunflower oil.
3. Arrange the sausages, halved tomatoes, mushrooms and bacon in the basket, ensuring they are not overcrowded.
4. Cook in the air fryer for 10 minutes.
5. Open the air fryer and carefully turn over the sausages and bacon to cook them evenly. Add the slices of black pudding to the basket.
6. Continue to cook for another 7-8 minutes until the sausages, bacon and black pudding are browned and cooked through.
7. In the meantime, prepare the baked beans in a saucepan over medium heat on your stove. Stir occasionally until thoroughly heated.
8. With around 2 minutes of cooking time left, crack the eggs into a separate greased fryer basket or aluminium foil shaped into a small boat to prevent the white from flowing off, then place it into the air fryer.
9. Check at the 2-minute mark; if the eggs are cooked to your liking, remove everything from the air fryer. If not, keep checking every 30 seconds until they're at your preferred doneness.
10. Season everything to taste with salt and pepper.
11. Serve the air-fried ingredients with the warmed baked beans, spreading everything out on a large plate or tray for a hearty full English breakfast.

NUTRITION FACTS PER 100G:
Energy: 190kcal | Protein: 9.5g | Total Fat: 14g | Saturated Fat: 5g |
Carbohydrates: 8g | Sugars: 3g | Dietary Fibre: 1.5g

SCOTTISH SCONE BITES

Servings: 12 Scone Bites | Difficulty: Medium | Temperature: 180 degrees Celsius |
Preparation Time: 15 minutes | Cooking Time: 10 minutes

INGREDIENTS:

- ✪ 225g self-raising flour
- ✪ 60g caster sugar
- ✪ 1/2 teaspoon bicarbonate of soda
- ✪ 1/4 teaspoon salt
- ✪ 60g unsalted butter, chilled and diced
- ✪ 125ml double cream
- ✪ 1 large egg
- ✪ 1 teaspoon vanilla extract
- ✪ 2 tablespoons milk for brushing

PREPARATION:

1. In a large bowl, combine the self-raising flour, caster sugar, bicarbonate of soda and salt.
2. Add the chilled, diced butter to the flour mix. Rub in the butter using your fingertips until the mixture looks like fine breadcrumbs.
3. In a separate bowl, combine the double cream, egg and vanilla extract. Stir well.
4. Gradually add the wet ingredients to the dry ingredients, mixing gently until a soft dough forms. Be careful not to overmix.
5. Turn the dough out onto a lightly floured surface and knead gently for a few seconds to bring it together.
6. Form the dough into small balls, approximately 1 inch in diameter.
7. Preheat your air fryer to 180 degrees Celsius.
8. Arrange the scone bites in the air fryer basket, leaving enough space between each one to allow for rising. You may need to cook them in batches.
9. Lightly brush the top of each scone bite with milk.
10. Air fry for 10 minutes, or until the scone bites are golden and well-risen.
11. Remove from the air fryer and let them cool on a wire rack before serving.

NUTRITION FACTS PER 100G:
Energy: 315kcal | Protein: 5.2g | Total Fat: 15.4g | Saturated Fat: 9.3g |
Carbohydrates: 37.8g | Sugars: 9.2g | Dietary Fibre: 1.2g

BREAKFAST EGG MUFFINS

Servings: 6 | Difficulty: Easy | Temperature: 180 degrees Celsius |
Preparation Time: 10 minutes | Cooking Time: 15 minutes

INGREDIENTS:

- 6 large eggs
- 100g cheddar cheese, grated
- 50g red bell pepper, diced
- 50g yellow bell pepper, diced
- 50g courgette, diced
- 4 spring onions, chopped
- 2 tablespoons double cream
- salt and pepper to taste

PREPARATION:

1. In a large bowl, crack the eggs and whisk them gently.
2. Add in the grated cheddar cheese, diced bell peppers, diced courgette, and chopped spring onions.
3. Pour in the double cream, add salt and pepper, then stir to combine all the ingredients.
4. Grease the air fryer basket or muffin cups if you have them and divide the mixture evenly among the cups.
5. Carefully place the basket or muffin cups in the air fryer.
6. Set the air fryer to 180 degrees Celsius and cook for about 15 minutes, or until the muffins are puffed up and golden.
7. Once done, remove the basket and let the muffins cool for a few minutes before serving.

NUTRITION FACTS PER 100G:
Energy: 209kcal | Protein: 13g | Total Fat: 15g | Saturated Fat: 6g |
Carbohydrates: 4g | Sugars: 2g | Dietary Fibre: 0.9g

KIPPERS AND TOAST SOLDIERS

Servings: 2 | Difficulty: Easy | Temperature: 180 degrees Celsius |
Preparation Time: 10 minutes | Cooking Time: 20 minutes

INGREDIENTS:

- ✪ 2 whole kippers (around 200g each)
- ✪ 4 tablespoons sunflower oil
- ✪ 4 thick slices of wholemeal bread
- ✪ 2 tablespoons unsalted butter
- ✪ salt to taste

PREPARATION:

1. Start by preheating your air fryer to 180 degrees Celsius.
2. Whilst the fryer is heating, wash the kippers under cold water, pat them dry with kitchen paper and then brush them lightly on both sides with 2 tablespoons of sunflower oil.
3. Once your air fryer has heated, place the kippers in the basket and cook for 10-12 minutes, and then flip them. Continue cooking for another 3-8 minutes, or until golden brown and cooked through.
4. While the kippers are cooking, it's time to prepare your toast soldiers. Lightly toast the wholemeal bread in a toaster or under a grill.
5. Next, brush each slice generously with melted unsalted butter, and then cut each slice into four 'soldiers'.
6. When your kippers are cooked, carefully remove them from the air fryer—watch out for any stray bones - and serve hot, sprinkled with a pinch of salt.
7. Serve your kippers alongside your freshly prepared toast soldiers.

NUTRITION FACTS PER 100G:
Energy: 230kcal | Protein: 15g | Total Fat: 15g | Saturated Fat: 4g |
Carbohydrates: 7g | Sugars: 1g | Dietary Fibre: 3g

WELSH RAREBIT BITES

Servings: 6 | Difficulty: Medium | Temperature: 180 degrees Celsius |
Preparation Time: 10 minutes | Cooking Time: 15 minutes

INGREDIENTS:

- 400g crusty bread, cut into bite-sized cubes
- 250g mature cheddar, grated
- 200ml ale
- 2 tablespoons Worcestershire sauce
- 2 tablespoons double cream
- 2 teaspoons English mustard
- 2 large free-range eggs

PREPARATION:

1. Preheat the air fryer to 180 degrees Celsius.
2. In a large bowl, combine the grated cheddar, ale, Worcestershire sauce, double cream, and English mustard. Stir well until combined.
3. Dip each bread cube into the cheese mixture, ensuring each piece is well coated. Place the coated bread cubes in one layer in the air fryer basket.
4. Cook the bread cubes for approximately 5 minutes, then open the air fryer and gently toss the bread to ensure an even cook.
5. Continue to cook for an additional 5 minutes, or until the bread is golden and the cheese is bubbling.
6. Whilst the bread is cooking, lightly beat the eggs in a separate bowl.
7. After 10 minutes of cooking time, remove the air fryer basket. Quickly but carefully dip each bread cube into the beaten eggs, then return them to the air fryer.
8. Cook the egg-coated bread for a further 3-5 minutes, until the egg coating is set and lightly browned.
9. Remove the Welsh rarebit bites from the air fryer using a heat-resistant tool, and allow to cool slightly before serving.

NUTRITION FACTS PER 100G:
Energy: 230kcal | Protein: 11g | Total Fat: 9g | Saturated Fat: 5g |
Carbohydrates: 20g | Sugars: 2g | Dietary Fibre: 1g

AIR-FRIED POTATO SCONES

Servings: 6 | Difficulty: Easy | Temperature: 200 degrees Celsius |
Preparation Time: 15 minutes | Cooking Time: 10 minutes

INGREDIENTS:

- 500g of white potatoes
- 50g of unsalted butter
- 100g of plain flour
- 1 teaspoon of salt
- 2 tablespoons of milk
- vegetable oil for misting

PREPARATION:

1. Start by peeling the potatoes and then chop them into chunks.
2. Place the chunks in a large saucepan, cover with water, add a pinch of salt, and bring to the boil.
3. Reduce the heat and let the potatoes simmer until they're tender. This should take about 10-15 minutes.
4. Drain the potatoes and allow them to cool.
5. Once potatoes have cooled, mash them until smooth in texture.
6. Melt butter and add it along with flour and salt to the mashed potatoes.
7. Add milk and knead the mixture until it forms a smooth dough.
8. Roll dough out to about 1cm thick.
9. Cut dough into circles using a round fluted cutter.
10. Preheat your air fryer to 200 degrees Celsius.
11. Mist both sides of the potato scones with vegetable oil and place them into the air fryer basket.
12. Cook scones in the air fryer for 5 minutes on each side till crispy and golden brown.
13. Your air-fried potato scones are ready to serve. Delight in them alone or with a hearty condiment!

NUTRITION FACTS PER 100G:
Energy: 123kcal | Protein: 2.3g | Total Fat: 3.5g | Saturated Fat: 2.2g |
Carbohydrates: 19g | Sugars: 0.8g | Dietary Fibre: 1.2g

BACON-WRAPPED ASPARAGUS SPEARS

Servings: 4 | Difficulty: Medium | Temperature: 180 degrees Celsius | Preparation Time: 15 minutes | Cooking Time: 10 minutes

INGREDIENTS:

- 16 fresh asparagus spears
- 100g streaky bacon
- salt to taste
- black pepper to taste
- 2 tablespoons olive oil
- 1 tablespoon lemon juice

PREPARATION:

1. Begin by washing and trimming the asparagus spears. Pat them dry with a kitchen towel.
2. Lay a strip of bacon on a flat surface. Place an asparagus spear at one end of the bacon strip. Roll it up tightly so that the asparagus is completely wrapped in bacon. Repeat this process for all the spears.
3. Once all the asparagus spears are wrapped in bacon, drizzle them with olive oil and rub it in to make sure each one is evenly coated.
4. Next, season the bacon-wrapped asparagus with salt and pepper to taste. Squeeze over the lemon juice to add a touch of acidity.
5. Preheat your air fryer to 180 degrees Celsius.
6. Arrange the prepared asparagus in the air fryer basket. Make sure they're in a single layer and not overlapping to ensure even cooking. You may have to cook them in batches depending on the size of your air fryer.
7. Cook the asparagus for about 10 minutes, or until the asparagus is tender and the bacon is crispy. Halfway through the cooking time, open the air fryer and shake the basket to ensure the bacon gets crispy on all sides.
8. Once they're done cooking, remove them from the air fryer and let them cool for a few minutes before serving.

NUTRITION FACTS PER 100G:
Energy: 115kcal | Protein: 7.1g | Total Fat: 8.5g | Saturated Fat: 2.5g | Carbohydrates: 3.2g | Sugars: 1.8g | Dietary Fibre: 1.5g

BAKED BEANS AND SAUSAGE CUPS

Servings: 6 | Difficulty: Medium | Temperature: 180 degrees Celsius |
Preparation Time: 20 minutes | Cooking Time: 12 minutes

INGREDIENTS:

- 400g canned baked beans
- 6 pre-cooked pork sausages, sliced into rounds
- 3 large eggs
- 60g grated mature cheddar cheese
- 3 tablespoons ketchup
- 2 tablespoons Worcestershire sauce
- 2 tablespoons wholegrain mustard
- 1 tablespoon olive oil
- 1 teaspoon hot chilli powder
- salt and pepper to taste
- 1 pack puff pastry sheets

PREPARATION:

1. Preheat the air fryer to 180 degrees Celsius.
2. Roll out the puff pastry on a floured surface and cut out the required number of circles to line a muffin tin. Gently press the pastry circles into the tin.
3. In a large bowl, mix the baked beans, sliced sausages, cheese, ketchup, Worcestershire sauce, mustard, and hot chilli powder. Mix well to ensure the ingredients are well combined.
4. Break the eggs into the bowl and stir well.
5. Season the mixture with salt and pepper, then mix again.
6. Generously spoon the baked beans and sausage mix into the puff pastry cups. Make sure each cup is filled to the brim.
7. Use a brush to apply a light layer of olive oil on top of each puff pastry cup. This will provide a beautiful golden colour and add some extra crunch.
8. Place the muffin tin in the air fryer and cook at 180 degrees for 12 minutes. The tops should be golden and crispy. If not, cook for an additional 2-3 minutes.
9. Once cooked, let them rest for a few minutes before serving. These can be enjoyed hot or cold.
10. Repeat the process with the remaining ingredients if needed.

NUTRITION FACTS PER 100G:
Energy: 254kcal | Protein: 10.4g | Total Fat: 16.7g | Saturated Fat: 6.2g |
Carbohydrates: 16.8g | Sugars: 3.0g | Dietary Fibre: 2.3g

TOMATO AND MUSHROOM TARTLETS

Servings: 6 | Difficulty: Medium | Temperature: 180 degrees Celsius | Preparation Time: 20 minutes | Cooking Time: 15 minutes

INGREDIENTS:

- 300g mixed mushrooms, finely chopped
- 200g cherry tomatoes, halved
- 2 tablespoons olive oil
- 1 onion, finely chopped
- 2 cloves of garlic, minced
- 1 teaspoon fresh thyme, chopped
- salt and pepper to taste
- 1 sheet ready-rolled puff pastry
- 200g cream cheese
- 1 egg, beaten

PREPARATION:

1. Preheat the air fryer to 180C.
2. Heat the olive oil in a pan over medium heat, add the onion and garlic, and cook until softened.
3. Add the chopped mushrooms, tomatoes, and thyme to the pan and cook for a further 5 minutes. Season with salt and pepper to taste.
4. While the vegetables are cooking, unroll the puff pastry and cut out 6 rounds to fit into the tartlet pans.
5. Divide the cream cheese evenly among the pastry rounds, spreading it generously.
6. Top each tartlet with the mushroom and tomato mixture.
7. Brush the edges of the tartlets with the beaten egg.
8. Place the tartlets into the air fryer basket and cook for 15 minutes or until golden and puffed up.
9. Allow the tartlets to cool for a few minutes before serving.

NUTRITION FACTS PER 100G:
Energy: 315kcal | Protein: 5.4g | Total Fat: 22.8g | Saturated Fat: 8g | Carbohydrates: 22.2g | Sugars: 2.8g | Dietary Fibre: 1.7g

PORRIDGE OAT BARS

Servings: 12 Bars | Difficulty: Easy | Temperature: 180 degrees Celsius |
Preparation Time: 15 minutes | Cooking Time: 20 minutes

INGREDIENTS:

- ✪ 200g porridge oats
- ✪ 100g unsalted butter
- ✪ 100g light brown sugar
- ✪ 2 tablespoons golden syrup
- ✪ 50g dried mixed fruit
- ✪ 1 teaspoon vanilla essence

PREPARATION:

1. In a saucepan, melt the unsalted butter, light brown sugar, and golden syrup together. Keep stirring it over a low heat until the sugar has fully dissolved.
2. Once the sugar has dissolved, pour in the vanilla essence and give it a good stir.
3. Next, add the porridge oats and dried mixed fruit to the saucepan. Mix everything together ensuring the oats and fruit are fully coated in the sweet, sticky mixture.
4. Line your air fryer basket with baking paper. Ensure it is cut to size so it fits neatly into the basket.
5. Transfer the oat mixture into the lined air fryer basket. Spread it evenly and press it down firmly so it holds together whilst cooking.
6. Set your air fryer to 180 degrees Celsius and cook the oat bars for 20 minutes, or until they are golden brown and firm to the touch.
7. Allow the oat bars to cool in the air fryer basket before removing. Once cool, use a sharp knife to cut them into 12 equal-sized bars.
8. These porridge oat bars can be stored in an airtight container for up to a week. They make a delicious, wholesome breakfast or snack on the go.

NUTRITION FACTS PER 100G:
Energy: 385kcal | Protein: 5.6g | Total Fat: 16g | Saturated Fat: 7.9g |
Carbohydrates: 54.6g | Sugars: 24g | Dietary Fibre: 3.7g

SPICED BREAKFAST QUINOA

Servings: 2 | Difficulty: Medium | Temperature: 175 degrees Celsius |
Preparation Time: 15 minutes | Cooking Time: 15 minutes

INGREDIENTS:

- 150g quinoa
- 240ml water
- 2 tablespoons olive oil
- 1/4 teaspoon ground cinnamon
- 1/4 teaspoon ground nutmeg
- 1 tablespoon honey
- 50g raisins
- 1 medium apple, chopped
- 50ml milk

PREPARATION:

1. Rinse the quinoa under cold water until the water runs clear. This is to remove any bitterness from the quinoa.
2. In a medium-sized bowl, combine the rinsed quinoa, water, olive oil, cinnamon, nutmeg, and salt. Stir well to ensure everything is evenly mixed.
3. Put the mixture into the air fryer basket and place the basket into the air fryer.
4. Set the air fryer to 175 degrees Celsius and set the timer for 15 minutes.
5. While the quinoa is cooking, combine the honey, raisins and chopped apple in a small bowl.
6. After the quinoa has cooked for 15 minutes, carefully remove the basket from the air fryer and gently mix in the honey, raisins, and apple. Place the basket back into the air fryer.
7. Cook the quinoa for an additional 5 minutes or until the apple is softened.
8. Once the cooking is complete, carefully remove the basket from the air fryer and let the quinoa cool slightly before serving.
9. Pour the milk over the quinoa before serving, adding extra sweetness and creaminess.

NUTRITION FACTS PER 100G:
Energy: 150kcal | Protein: 4.5g | Total Fat: 3.2g | Saturated Fat: 0.5g |
Carbohydrates: 24g | Sugars: 9g | Dietary Fibre: 2.6g

AIR-FRIED BERRY AND YOGHURT TARTS

Servings: 4 | Difficulty: Medium | Temperature: 180 degrees Celsius |
Preparation Time: 20 minutes | Cooking Time: 12 minutes

INGREDIENTS:

- 4 pre-made tart shells (about 4-inch size)
- 400g Greek yoghurt
- 300g mixed berries (blueberries, raspberries, strawberries)
- 2 tablespoons honey
- 1 teaspoon vanilla extract
- 1 tablespoon icing sugar (for dusting)
- mint leaves for garnish (optional)

PREPARATION:

1. Preheat the air fryer to 180 degrees Celsius.
2. In a mixing bowl, combine Greek yoghurt, honey, and vanilla extract. Mix until smooth.
3. Wash and dry the mixed berries. If using strawberries, chop them into smaller pieces to match the size of the other berries.
4. Spoon the Greek yoghurt mixture into each pre-made tart shell, filling up to 2/3 full.
5. Place a variety of mixed berries on top of the yoghurt filling in each tart shell.
6. Carefully place the filled tart shells into the air fryer basket, ensuring they do not touch each other.
7. Air-fry for 10-12 minutes or until the edges of the tart shells are golden brown.
8. Carefully remove the tarts from the air fryer and let them cool for a few minutes.
9. Dust the tops with a light coating of icing sugar and garnish with mint leaves if using.
10. Serve immediately, or refrigerate for later use.

NUTRITION FACTS PER 100G:
Energy: 180kcal | Protein: 6g | Fat: 8g | Saturated Fat: 4g |
Carbohydrates: 22g | Sugars: 14g | Dietary Fibre: 1g

LEMON AND POPPY SEED MUFFINS

Servings: 12 muffins | Difficulty: Medium | Temperature: 180 degrees Celsius | Preparation Time: 15 minutes | Cooking Time: 15 minutes

INGREDIENTS:

- 175g plain flour
- 150g caster sugar
- 1.5 tablespoons poppy seeds
- zest of 2 lemons
- 2 tablespoons lemon juice
- 120ml milk
- 60ml vegetable oil
- 2 large eggs
- 1 teaspoon baking powder
- 1/2 teaspoon bicarbonate of soda
- 1/4 teaspoon salt
- 1 teaspoon pure vanilla extract

PREPARATION:

1. In a large bowl, combine the plain flour, caster sugar, poppy seeds, baking powder, bicarbonate of soda, and salt. Stir until well mixed.
2. In another bowl, whisk together the milk, vegetable oil, eggs, lemon zest, lemon juice, and vanilla extract.
3. Gradually add the liquid ingredients to the dry ones, stirring as you go along. Stir well until the mixture is properly combined and smooth, making sure no lumps of flour remain.
4. Using the air fryer basket, divide the muffin mixture among the 12 muffin spots. Remember, these baskets should not be overcrowded, so you may need to do it in batches depending on the size of your air fryer.
5. Set your air fryer to 180 degrees Celsius. Cook the muffins for about 15 minutes, or until a toothpick inserted comes out clean and they are golden brown on top.
6. Allow the muffins to cool thoroughly before removing them from the air fryer. Once cooled, they are ready to serve.

NUTRITION FACTS PER 100G:
Energy: 198kcal | Protein: 3.5g | Total Fat: 7.6g | Saturated Fat: 1.2g | Carbohydrates: 29.7g | Sugars: 15.8g | Dietary Fibre: 0.9g

CINNAMON FRENCH TOAST

Servings: 4 | Difficulty: Easy | Temperature: 180 degrees Celsius |
Preparation Time: 15 minutes | Cooking Time: 10 minutes

INGREDIENTS:

- 8 slices of thick-cut bread
- 3 large eggs
- 240ml milk
- 2 tablespoons caster sugar
- 2 teaspoons ground cinnamon
- 1 teaspoon pure vanilla extract
- pinch of salt
- 4 tablespoons unsalted butter, melted
- icing sugar for dusting
- 100ml maple syrup

PREPARATION:

1. Preheat the air fryer to 180 degrees Celsius.
2. In a large shallow bowl, whisk together eggs, milk, caster sugar, cinnamon, vanilla extract and salt.
3. Dip each slice of bread into the egg mixture, ensuring each side is well coated.
4. Brush the air fryer basket with a portion of the melted butter.
5. Arrange as many slices of the bread that can fit in a single layer in the air fryer basket.
6. Cook for 5 minutes, then flip the bread slices, brush with more melted butter, and cook for another 5 minutes, or until golden and crisp.
7. Repeat steps 4 to 6 with the remaining slices of bread.
8. Serve the French toast dusted with icing sugar and a drizzle of maple syrup.

NUTRITION FACTS PER 100G:
Energy: 230kcal | Protein: 7.0g | Total Fat: 11.0g | Saturated Fat: 5.0g |
Carbohydrates: 27.0g | Sugars: 9.5g | Dietary Fibre: 0.8g

CRISPY GRANOLA CLUSTERS

Servings: 6 | Difficulty: Medium | Temperature: 160 degrees Celsius |
Preparation Time: 10 minutes | Cooking Time: 15 minutes

INGREDIENTS:

- 300g of old-fashioned oats
- 120g of chopped nuts (almonds, walnuts, pecans)
- 3 tablespoons of light brown sugar
- 1/2 teaspoon of ground cinnamon
- 1/4 teaspoon of salt
- 120ml of honey
- 2 tablespoons of extra virgin olive oil
- 1 teaspoon of vanilla extract
- 150g of dried fruits (cranberries, apricots, raisins)

PREPARATION:

1. Mix the oats, chopped nuts, light brown sugar, ground cinnamon, and salt in a bowl until all ingredients are evenly combined.
2. In a separate bowl, whisk together honey, extra virgin olive oil, and vanilla extract.
3. Pour the wet ingredients over the dry ingredients and stir until every oat and nut piece is thoroughly coated.
4. Preheat the air fryer to 160 degrees Celsius and line the air fryer basket with air fryer parchment paper.
5. Transfer the oat mixture into the air fryer basket, spread it evenly and press it down into a flat layer.
6. Cook for about 15 minutes until golden brown, shaking the basket every 5 minutes to ensure the granola cooks evenly and doesn't burn.
7. Turn off the air fryer and let the granola cool completely in the basket. It will continue to harden as it cools.
8. Once cooled, break the granola into clusters and add the dried fruits.
9. Store the granola clusters in an airtight container at room temperature or serve as desired.

NUTRITION FACTS PER 100G:
Energy: 397kcal | Protein: 9.8g | Total Fat: 14.2g | Saturated Fat: 1.8g |
Carbohydrates: 64.2g | Sugars: 25.6g | Dietary Fibre: 7.9g

BLUEBERRY AND BANANA PANCAKES

Servings: 4 | Difficulty: Easy | Temperature: 180 degrees Celsius | Preparation Time: 10 minutes | Cooking Time: 15 minutes

INGREDIENTS:

- 150g self-raising flour
- 1 ripe banana
- 125ml whole milk
- 2 tablespoons caster sugar
- 1 large egg
- 1 tablespoon sunflower oil
- 100g fresh blueberries
- a pinch of salt
- maple syrup, for serving

PREPARATION:

1. Get a mixing bowl, mash the ripe banana and set it aside for a moment.
2. In a separate bowl, combine the self-raising flour, caster sugar, and a pinch of salt.
3. Make a well in the middle of the flour mixture. Pour in the egg, milk, and mashed banana.
4. Use a whisk to combine the ingredients into a smooth pancake batter.
5. Add the fresh blueberries and stir gently to incorporate them.
6. Preheat your air fryer to 180 degrees Celsius for five minutes.
7. Brush the air fryer basket lightly with sunflower oil to prevent the pancakes from sticking.
8. Pour enough batters into the air fryer basket to make a pancake about 10cm in diameter. Do not overfill as the pancake needs space to expand.
9. Cook each pancake in the air fryer for 7 to 8 minutes or until golden brown on both sides.
10. Remove the pancake from the air fryer and keep it warm. Repeat the process with the remaining batter.
11. Serve the blueberry and banana pancakes immediately, drizzled with a generous amount of maple syrup.

NUTRITION FACTS PER 100G:
Energy: 154kcal | Protein: 3.8g | Total Fat: 3.4g | Saturated Fat: 0.9g | Carbohydrates: 26.2g | Sugars: 10.5g | Dietary Fibre: 1.2g

SAVOURY CHEDDAR AND CHIVE MUFFINS

Servings: 12 Muffins | Difficulty: Medium | Temperature: 190 degrees Celsius | Preparation Time: 15 minutes | Cooking Time: 15 minutes

INGREDIENTS:

- 190g plain flour
- 150g mature cheddar cheese, grated
- 2 tablespoons fresh chives, chopped
- 1 tablespoon sugar
- 2 teaspoons baking powder
- 1/2 teaspoon salt
- 240ml milk
- 1 large egg
- 90ml vegetable oil

PREPARATION:

1. In a large bowl, combine the plain flour, grated cheddar cheese, chopped chives, sugar, baking powder, and salt.
2. In a separate bowl, whisk together the milk, egg, and vegetable oil.
3. Slowly add the wet ingredients to the dry ingredients. Mix gently until the flour is moistened.
4. Once the batter is mixed, divide the mixture evenly into silicone muffin cups, filling each cup nearly to the top.
5. Place the silicone cups with the muffin mixture in the air fryer basket. You may need to do this in batches depending on the size of your air fryer.
6. Set the air fryer temperature to 190 degrees Celsius and cook for approximately 15 minutes, or until the muffins are golden brown and firm to touch.
7. Remove from the air fryer and allow them to cool slightly before enjoying your savoury cheddar and chive muffins.

NUTRITION FACTS PER 100G:
Energy: 240kcal | Protein: 7.5g | Total Fat: 9.5g | Saturated Fat: 4.6g | Carbohydrates: 28.8g | Sugars: 3.5g | Dietary Fibre: 0.7g

CRISPY BREAKFAST POTATOES

Servings: 4 | Difficulty: Easy | Temperature: 200 degrees Celsius |
Preparation Time: 10 minutes | Cooking Time: 30 minutes

INGREDIENTS:

- 600g new potatoes
- 2 tablespoons olive oil
- 1 tablespoon paprika
- 1 tablespoon garlic powder
- salt to taste
- freshly ground black pepper to taste
- 2 tablespoons fresh parsley, finely chopped

PREPARATION:

1. Rinse the new potatoes and cut them into halves or quarters, depending on their size.
2. Place the cut potatoes in a large bowl, add the olive oil, paprika, garlic powder, salt, and freshly ground black pepper. Mix well until the potatoes are evenly coated.
3. Preheat the air fryer to 200 degrees Celsius.
4. Arrange the potatoes in a single layer in the air fryer basket. Depending on the size of your air fryer, you may need to cook in batches.
5. Cook the potatoes in the air fryer for 15 minutes, then give them a shake from the basket. This helps them to cook evenly.
6. After shaking, cook the potatoes for another 15 minutes until they are crispy and golden brown.
7. Once cooked, remove the potatoes from the air fryer and sprinkle them with the freshly chopped parsley.
8. Serve the crispy breakfast potatoes piping hot and enjoy as they are or with a ketchup dip.

NUTRITION FACTS PER 100G:
Energy: 108kcal | Protein: 2g | Total Fat: 4g | Saturated Fat: 0.5g |
Carbohydrates: 16g | Sugars: 0.8g | Dietary Fibre: 2g

IRISH SODA BREAD SLICES

Servings: 6 | Difficulty: Easy | Temperature: 160 degrees Celsius |
Preparation Time: 60 minutes | Cooking Time: 10 minutes

INGREDIENTS:

- 450g plain flour
- 1 teaspoon baking soda
- 1 teaspoon table salt
- 400ml buttermilk
- 2 tablespoons granulated sugar
- 2 tablespoons unsalted butter, melted

PREPARATION:

1. In a large mixing bowl, sift together the flour, baking soda, and salt.
2. Stir in the sugar.
3. Gradually pour in the buttermilk, constantly mixing until a soft dough is formed.
4. Turn the dough onto a floured surface and knead slightly until it is smooth and round.
5. Using a sharp knife, cut the dough into 6 equal slices.
6. Brush each slice with melted butter.
7. Put the slices of dough in the air fryer basket, taking care not to crowd them. They should have enough space for air to circulate around each piece.
8. Set the air fryer to 160 degrees Celsius and cook for 10 minutes. Keep an eye on the fryer as temperatures can vary and it might be necessary to adjust the cooking time.
9. Test the bread with a toothpick after 10 minutes. If the toothpick comes out clean, the bread is done. If dough sticks to the toothpick, return the bread to the fryer for an additional 2-3 minutes and test again.
10. Once done, remove the slices and let cool on a wire rack.

NUTRITION FACTS PER 100G:
Energy: 252kcal | Protein: 6.5g | Total Fat: 2.5g | Saturated Fat: 1.5g |
Carbohydrates: 49g | Sugars: 3g | Dietary Fibre: 1.7g

Chapter 2:
Nibbles and Starters (20 recipes)

PRAWN COCKTAIL CUPS

Servings: 4 | Difficulty: Medium | Temperature: 200 degrees Celsius |
Preparation Time: 20 minutes | Cooking Time: 10 minutes

INGREDIENTS:

- 500g fresh prawns, peeled and deveined
- 4 large soft tortilla wraps
- 200g iceberg lettuce, shredded
- 100ml mayonnaise
- 100ml tomato ketchup
- 1 tablespoon Worcestershire sauce
- 1 tablespoon lemon juice
- a pinch of paprika
- salt to taste
- freshly ground black pepper to taste

PREPARATION:

1. Preheat your air fryer to 200 degrees Celsius.
2. Press your large soft tortilla wraps into the cups of a silicon muffin tin to form cup shapes.
3. Once you have your tortilla cups ready, place the muffin tin into the air fryer basket. Fry them for about 5 minutes, or until they're crispy and golden.
4. In a large bowl, combine the mayonnaise, tomato ketchup, Worcestershire sauce, lemon juice, and a small pinch of paprika. Season the mix with salt and freshly ground black pepper to taste. Set this sauce aside for a while.
5. Add the prawns to the air fryer basket, ensuring they're evenly distributed and not overlapping to ensure they cook evenly.
6. Cook the prawns for about 3-4 minutes, then turn them and fry for another 3-4 minutes. The prawns will be ready when they turn a rich, pink colour.
7. Allow the prawns to cool for a few minutes before adding them to the sauce you prepared earlier. Stir well to ensure all the prawns are well coated.
8. To serve, divide the shredded lettuce between the cooled, crispy tortilla cups, then top with the prawn and sauce mixture. Serve immediately.

NUTRITION FACTS PER 100G:
Energy: 170kcal | Protein: 8.5g | Total Fat: 8.2g | Saturated Fat: 1.4g |
Carbohydrates: 13.4g | Sugars: 2.8g | Dietary Fibre: 0.9g

STILTON AND BROCCOLI SOUP SHOTS

Servings: 8 | Difficulty: Medium | Temperature: 180 degrees Celsius |
Preparation Time: 15 minutes | Cooking Time: 25 minutes

INGREDIENTS:

- 200g of broccoli, cut into small florets
- 50g of Stilton cheese, crumbled
- 500ml of vegetable stock
- 1 small white onion, diced
- 2 cloves of garlic, minced
- 140ml double cream
- 1 tablespoon of olive oil
- freshly ground black pepper to taste
- a pinch of salt

PREPARATION:

1. Preheat the air fryer to 180 degrees Celsius.
2. After lightly coating the broccoli florets with olive oil, place them in the air fryer and cook for around 10 minutes or until they are slightly crispy and have a nice roasted colour.
3. Meanwhile, heat olive oil in a large pan over medium heat, add the diced onion and minced garlic and sauté until they become tender and fragrant.
4. Once the broccoli is ready, add it to the pan with onions and garlic, then gradually pour in the vegetable stock. Bring this to a brief simmer.
5. Crumble the Stilton cheese into the soup and stir until the cheese has melted completely and is well incorporated with the soup.
6. Slowly stir in the double cream and continue to heat the mixture on a low heat for an additional 5 minutes. Season the soup with salt and pepper.
7. Finally, using a handheld or countertop blender, blend the soup until it's smooth. Be careful to let the soup cool slightly before this step to avoid potential splashing.
8. Serve the soup in small glasses or shot glasses for a creative, party-ready presentation.

NUTRITION FACTS PER 100G:
Energy: 150kcal | Protein: 3.1g | Total Fat: 11g | Saturated Fat: 5.2g |
Carbohydrates: 9.2g | Sugars: 2.5g | Dietary Fibre: 1.7g

SCOTCH EGGS

Servings: 4 | Difficulty: Medium | Temperature: 200 degrees Celsius |
Preparation Time: 20 minutes | Cooking Time: 12 minutes

INGREDIENTS:

- 4 large eggs, pre-boiled
- 8 good quality pork sausages
- 100g plain flour
- 2-3 beaten eggs
- 200g bread crumbs
- 1 tablespoon dried oregano
- 1 tablespoon dried thyme
- 1 tablespoon garlic powder
- 1 tablespoon onion powder
- salt, to taste
- freshly ground black pepper, to taste
- a handful of freshly chopped parsley

PREPARATION:

1. Pre-cook the eggs to a hard-boil, allow them to cool, then peel and set aside.
2. Cut open the sausages and remove the meat, placing it in a large bowl.
3. Add the oregano, thyme, garlic powder, onion powder, chopped parsley, salt and pepper to the sausage meat. Mix until well combined.
4. Flatten out a piece of sausage meat in your hand and wrap it around one of the pre-cooked eggs, covering completely. Repeat with the remaining eggs.
5. In three separate bowls, place the flour, beaten eggs, and bread crumbs.
6. Roll each sausage-covered egg in the flour, then do an egg wash by dipping into the beaten eggs, and finally, roll in the breadcrumbs, ensuring each one is thoroughly coated.
7. Preheat the air fryer to 200 degrees Celsius.
8. Place the Scotch eggs in the air fryer basket, ensuring they do not touch and have space to cook evenly.
9. Cook at 200 degrees Celsius for 12 minutes, or until golden brown.
10. Remove the Scotch eggs from the air fryer and allow them to cool slightly before serving.

NUTRITION FACTS PER 100G:
Energy: 310kcal | Protein: 12g | Total Fat: 22g | Saturated Fat: 8g |
Carbohydrates: 13g | Sugars: 1g | Dietary Fibre: 1g

AIR-FRIED HAGGIS BALLS

Servings: 4 | Difficulty: Medium | Temperature: 180 degrees Celsius |
Preparation Time: 30 minutes | Cooking Time: 15 minutes

INGREDIENTS:

- ✪ 450g haggis, cooked, cooled, and crumbled
- ✪ 3 tablespoons plain flour
- ✪ 2 large eggs, beaten
- ✪ 150g golden breadcrumbs
- ✪ vegetable oil, for greasing
- ✪ sea salt and black pepper to taste
- ✪ 2 tablespoons tomato sauce for dip

PREPARATION:

1. Start by preheating your air fryer to 180 degrees Celsius, then lightly grease the frying basket with the vegetable oil.
2. Take the chilled and crumbled haggis and form small, roughly 2cm in diameter, round shape balls.
3. Place the plain flour, beaten eggs, and breadcrumbs in separate bowls.
4. Season the flour with a pinch of sea salt and black pepper to give it extra flavour.
5. One by one, roll the haggis balls in the flour until fully coated, then dip each ball into the beaten eggs, followed by a good roll in the breadcrumbs. Ensure every ball is fully coated with each ingredient.
6. Place the coated balls in the greased air-fryer basket, ensuring there is enough space between them for the air to circulate properly.
7. Air-fry the haggis balls for 15 minutes, or until they turn crispy and golden.
8. Once done, carefully remove the haggis balls from the air fryer, allow them to cool for a few minutes before serving with tomato sauce for dipping.

NUTRITION FACTS PER 100G:
Energy: 290kcal | Protein: 12g | Total Fat: 18g | Saturated Fat: 7g |
Carbohydrates: 20g | Sugars: 1g | Dietary Fibre: 1g

MINI CORNISH PASTIES

Servings: 6 | Difficulty: Medium | Temperature: 180 degrees Celsius | Preparation Time: 45 minutes | Cooking Time: 15 minutes

INGREDIENTS:

- 125g plain flour
- 60g unsalted butter
- pinch of salt
- 3-4 tablespoons cold water
- 100g skirt steak, finely chopped
- 50g swede, finely diced
- 50g potato, finely diced
- 1/4 white onion, finely chopped
- 1 teaspoon Worcestershire sauce
- salt and pepper to taste
- 1 egg, beaten

PREPARATION:

1. Start by making the pastry. Put the flour, butter, and a pinch of salt in a food processor and blend until the mixture looks like breadcrumbs.
2. Slowly add water, 1 tablespoon at a time, until the mixture comes together into a dough. Turn it out onto a lightly floured surface and knead briefly until smooth.
3. Roll out the dough thinly and use a round cutter to make 6 circles, re-rolling the dough as necessary.
4. Next, prepare the filling by mixing together the steak, swede, potato, and onion in a bowl. Add the Worcestershire sauce, and season with salt and pepper.
5. Divide the filling between the circles of dough, leaving a border around the edge. Brush the edges with a little water, then fold over and pinch to seal, creating a semi-circular pasty.
6. Place the pasties on a baking tray lined with baking parchment.
7. Brush the tops of the pasties with the beaten egg to glaze.
8. Preheat the air fryer to 180 degrees Celsius.
9. Place the tray with the pasties in the air fryer and cook for approximately 15 minutes, until golden brown and crisp.
10. Remove the pasties from the air fryer and let them cool for a few minutes before serving.

NUTRITION FACTS PER 100G:
Energy: 150kcal | Protein: 6.8g | Total Fat: 8.5g | Saturated Fat: 3.6g | Carbohydrates: 12g | Sugars: 0.9g | Dietary Fibre: 0.8g

SAUSAGE ROLLS

Servings: 12 | Difficulty: Easy | Temperature: 190 degrees Celsius |
Preparation Time: 20 minutes | Cooking Time: 15 minutes

INGREDIENTS:

- 500g pork sausage meat
- 320g pre-rolled puff pastry
- 1 large egg
- 2 tablespoons breadcrumbs
- 1 tablespoon dried sage
- 1 tablespoon dried thyme
- salt and pepper to taste

PREPARATION:

1. Preheat the air fryer to 190 degrees Celsius.
2. Lay out the pre-rolled puff pastry and cut it into 12 equal squares.
3. In a bowl, combine the sausage meat, breadcrumbs, sage, thyme, salt and pepper. Mix until everything is evenly distributed.
4. Form the sausage mixture into 12 equal sausage shapes.
5. Lay one sausage shape on each square of puff pastry. Roll the pastry around the sausage, leaving the ends open. Repeat for all the squares.
6. In a separate bowl, beat the egg. Use a brush or your fingers to spread a bit of the beaten egg along the edge of each pastry square to help seal the roll.
7. Transfer the sausage rolls onto the frying basket, making sure to leave space around each one so the air can circulate.
8. Cook for 15 minutes, or until the pastry is golden and the sausage is fully cooked.
9. Let the sausage rolls cool for a few minutes before serving. They should be handled with care as they will be extremely hot.

NUTRITION FACTS PER 100G:
Energy: 300kcal | Protein: 9g | Total Fat: 23g | Saturated Fat: 7g |
Carbohydrates: 14g | Sugars: 0.5g | Dietary Fibre: 0.8g

PLOUGHMAN'S SKEWERS

Servings: 6 | Difficulty: Easy | Temperature: 190 degrees Celsius | Preparation Time: 60 minutes | Cooking Time: 8 minutes

INGREDIENTS:

- 6 large wooden skewers
- 180g of sharp cheddar cheese, cut into cubes
- 240g of cooked ham, cut into cubes
- 360g of cherry tomatoes
- 1 cucumber, cut into chunks
- 2 red apples, diced
- 1 tablespoon of vegetable oil
- 1 teaspoon of salt
- 1 teaspoon of black pepper

PREPARATION:

1. Start by prepping all your ingredients. Cut the cheese, ham, cucumbers, and apples into bite-sized cubes and wash the cherry tomatoes.
2. Thread the ingredients onto the skewers. Following this order will provide a balanced flavour; first tomato, then cheese, then ham, followed by cucumber and lastly, the apple. Repeat this process until the skewer is full. Try to leave a small space at the bottom to easily hold the skewers.
3. Once done, lightly brush the skewers with some vegetable oil, then season with salt and pepper.
4. Preheat your air fryer at 190 degrees Celsius.
5. Once it's heated, carefully place the skewers in the fryer!
6. Cook the skewers for about 8 minutes, or until the cheese is slightly melted and everything is heated through.
7. Once done, carefully remove the skewers from the air fryer using a pair of tongs.
8. Allow the skewers to cool for a few minutes before serving.

NUTRITION FACTS PER 100G:
Energy: 149kcal | Protein: 10.5g | Total Fat: 8.5g | Saturated Fat: 3.7g | Carbohydrates: 8g | Sugars: 6g | Dietary Fibre: 1.1g

VEGETABLE SAMOSAS

Servings: 16 samosas | Difficulty: Medium | Temperature: 200 degrees Celsius |
Preparation Time: 30 minutes | Cooking Time: 15 minutes

INGREDIENTS:

- 2 medium potatoes (approximately 300g), peeled and cubed
- 100g frozen peas
- 2 tablespoons sunflower oil
- 1 medium onion, finely chopped
- 2 cloves of garlic, minced
- 2 teaspoons freshly grated ginger
- 2 teaspoons curry powder
- 1 teaspoon garam masala
- 1 teaspoon cumin seeds
- salt to taste
- 16 ready-made samosa wrappers
- 3 tablespoons flour mixed with water to make a paste

PREPARATION:

1. Boil the peas and potatoes until they become soft. This should take about 15 minutes. Drain them and set aside.
2. Heat the oil in a frying pan over medium heat, add the cumin seeds and let it splutter for a few seconds.
3. Add the onion and cook until translucent for about 5 minutes.
4. Stir in the garlic, ginger, curry powder, and garam masala. Cook this mixture for a minute until the spices are fragrant.
5. Add the boiled peas and potatoes to this mixture. Mash them slightly with the back of your spoon while stirring to mix well with the spices. Season with salt according to taste, then set aside to cool.
6. Take a samosa wrapper, place a spoonful of the filling on the wrapper. Fold the wrapper into a triangular shape around the mixture and seal the edges with flour paste.
7. Repeat this with the remaining wrappers until all the filling is used.
8. Preheat the air fryer to 200 degrees Celsius.
9. Place the samosas in the air fryer basket in a single layer and cook for 10-15 minutes or until the samosas are golden and crispy.
10. Serve your vegetable samosas hot with your favourite type of sauce.

NUTRITION FACTS PER 100G:
Energy: 138kcal | Protein: 3.1g | Total Fat: 4.7g | Saturated Fat: 0.6g |
Carbohydrates: 20.8g | Sugars: 1.7g | Dietary Fibre: 3.1g

SPICED CAULIFLOWER WINGS

Servings: 4 | Difficulty: Easy | Temperature: 200 degrees Celsius |
Preparation Time: 10 minutes | Cooking Time: 20 minutes

INGREDIENTS:

- 1 large head of cauliflower (cut into florets) 600g
- 3 tablespoons olive oil
- 4 tablespoons plain flour
- 240ml water
- 2 teaspoons garlic granules
- 1 teaspoon paprika
- 1 teaspoon ground coriander
- 1/2 teaspoon black pepper
- 1/2 teaspoon salt
- 4 tablespoons hot sauce
- 2 tablespoons honey
- 4 tablespoons unsalted butter, melted

PREPARATION:

1. Preheat your air fryer to 200 degrees Celsius.
2. In a large bowl, mix together the flour, water, garlic granules, paprika, coriander, black pepper and salt to create a batter.
3. Toss the cauliflower florets into the batter, making sure each piece is evenly coated.
4. Arrange the coated cauliflower in your preheated air fryer. Make sure they're spread out and not touching, you may need to do this in batches.
5. Cook for 15 minutes, then shake the basket to turn the florets and cook for another 5 minutes until crispy and golden brown.
6. While the cauliflower is cooking, mix together the hot sauce, honey, and melted butter in a separate bowl.
7. Once the cauliflower is done cooking, carefully remove it from the air fryer and toss in the hot sauce mixture until each piece is fully coated.
8. Return the coated cauliflower to the air fryer and cook for another 2-3 minutes to let the sauce set.
9. Once the time is up, remove the cauliflower wings from the air fryer and serve hot.

NUTRITION FACTS PER 100G:
Energy: 115kcal | Protein: 2.3g | Total Fat: 7.5g | Saturated Fat: 2.2g |
Carbohydrates: 9.2g | Sugars: 4.0g | Dietary Fibre: 2.5g

COURGETTE AND CHEESE FRITTERS

Servings: 4 | Difficulty: Medium | Temperature: 180 Degrees Celsius |
Preparation Time: 15 minutes | Cooking Time: 15 minutes

INGREDIENTS:

- 2 large courgettes (approximately 600g)
- 100g cheddar cheese, grated
- 100g self-raising flour
- 2 large eggs
- 1 tablespoon dried oregano
- 2 tablespoons olive oil
- 1 teaspoon garlic granules
- salt and pepper to taste

PREPARATION:

1. Begin with the courgettes. Wash the courgettes thoroughly, then grate them into a bowl, discarding any excess water.
2. To the same bowl, add the grated Cheddar cheese, self-raising flour, eggs, dried oregano, and garlic granules.
3. Thoroughly mix all the ingredients until you achieve a batter-like consistency.
4. Preheat the air fryer to 180 degrees Celsius.
5. Form the courgette mixture into small fritters, ensuring to flatten them slightly so they can cook evenly.
6. Using a brush, lightly grease the base of the air fryer with 1 tablespoon of olive oil.
7. In batches, place the fritters in the air fryer, taking care not to overcrowd the basket.
8. Cook the fritters for 8 minutes, then flip them over and cook for a further 7 minutes or until golden brown.
9. Repeat the process with the remaining courgette mixture.
10. Season the cooked fritters with salt and pepper to taste.

NUTRITION FACTS PER 100G:
Energy: 129kcal | Protein: 6.5g | Total Fat: 6.2g | Saturated Fat: 2.2g |
Carbohydrates: 10.2g | Sugars: 2.0g | Dietary Fibre: 1.8g

MINI SHEPHERD'S PIES

Servings: 4-6 | Difficulty: Medium | Temperature: 180 degrees Celsius | Preparation Time: 25 minutes | Cooking Time: 15 minutes

INGREDIENTS:

- 350g minced lamb
- 200g diced carrots
- 100g peas
- 1 diced onion
- 2 cloves of garlic, minced
- 1 tablespoon tomato puree
- 150ml beef stock
- 800g potatoes, peeled and diced
- 3 tablespoons butter
- 100ml double cream
- 50g cheddar cheese, grated
- salt and black pepper to taste

PREPARATION:

1. Heat a large pan over medium heat and add the minced lamb. Cook until brown and fully cooked. Drain the excess fat.
2. Add the onions, carrots, garlic, and peas to the pan with the lamb. Stir and cook until the vegetables are tender.
3. Mix in the tomato puree and beef stock. Reduce the heat and let the mixture simmer for about 10 minutes, stirring occasionally, until the stock has reduced.
4. While the lamb mixture is simmering, boil the diced potatoes in a separate pot until they're tender. Drain the water and mash the potatoes along with the butter, double cream, cheese, salt, and black pepper until smooth.
5. Preheat your air fryer to 180 degrees Celsius.
6. Spoon the lamb mixture into 4-6 mini baking dishes or ramekins, filling about 2/3 of each dish.
7. Top the lamb mixture with the mashed potatoes, spreading them out to completely cover the top.
8. Place the mini pies in the air fryer basket, being sure to not overcrowd them.
9. Cook in the air fryer for 15 minutes, or until the tops are golden brown.
10. Allow to cool for a few minutes before serving.

NUTRITION FACTS PER 100G:
Energy: 122kcal | Protein: 7.3g | Total Fat: 6.8g | Saturated Fat: 3.3g | Carbohydrates: 8.8g | Sugars: 1.8g | Dietary Fibre: 1.4g

SWEETCORN AND CORIANDER FRITTERS

Servings: 4 | Difficulty: Easy | Temperature: 180 degrees Celsius |
Preparation Time: 15 minutes | Cooking Time: 10 minutes

INGREDIENTS:

- 100g sweetcorn
- handful of fresh coriander, chopped
- 80g plain flour
- 1 teaspoon baking powder
- 1 large egg
- 100ml milk
- 1 tablespoon vegetable oil
- salt and pepper, to taste

PREPARATION:

1. In a bowl, combine the sweetcorn and chopped coriander. Add in the flour and baking powder, and mix well.
2. In a separate bowl, whisk the egg and milk together. Pour this mixture into the sweetcorn and coriander mixture. Stir to combine until a batter forms. Season with salt and pepper.
3. Preheat your air fryer at 180 degrees Celsius.
4. While the air fryer is heating, use a tablespoon to scoop the batter and form little fritters.
5. Carefully place the fritters in the air fryer basket in a single layer making sure they do not touch. You may need to do this in batches depending on the size of your air fryer.
6. Brush the tops of the fritters with a little vegetable oil.
7. Cook in the air fryer for 5 minutes. After 5 minutes, carefully flip the fritters over using a spatula, and brush the other sides with more oil.
8. Continue cooking for another 5 minutes, or until golden brown and crispy.
9. Allow the fritters to cool for a couple of minutes before serving. Repeat with the remaining batches if necessary.
10. Serve the fritters warm with a dip of your choice.

NUTRITION FACTS PER 100G:
Energy: 90kcal | Protein: 3g | Total Fat: 2.2g | Saturated Fat: 0.5g |
Carbohydrate: 14g | Sugars: 3g | Dietary Fibre: 2.4g

CHILLI AND LIME CHICKEN WINGS

Servings: 4 | Difficulty: Medium | Temperature: 190 degrees Celsius |
Preparation Time: 15 minutes | Cooking Time: 20 minutes

INGREDIENTS:

- ✪ 1kg chicken wings
- ✪ 4 tablespoons olive oil
- ✪ 2 chilli peppers (chopped)
- ✪ zest and juice of 2 limes
- ✪ 4 cloves garlic
- ✪ 2 tablespoons honey
- ✪ salt to taste
- ✪ 1 teaspoon black pepper
- ✪ handful of fresh coriander (chopped)

PREPARATION:

1. Place the chicken wings in a large bowl. Set aside.
2. In a smaller bowl, combine the olive oil, chilli peppers, lime zest, lime juice, minced garlic, honey, salt, and black pepper. Stir everything until it's well combined.
3. Pour the chilli-lime mixture over the chicken wings. Using your hands, toss the wings in the mixture, making sure each wing is thoroughly coated.
4. Cover the bowl with cling film and let it marinate in the refrigerator for at least 1 hour. If you have the time, you can leave it to marinate overnight for a deeper flavour.
5. Preheat your air fryer at 190 degrees Celsius.
6. Arrange the chicken wings in the air fryer basket, making sure not to overcrowd it. You may have to cook in batches depending on the size of your air fryer.
7. Cook the wings for 20 minutes or until they are crispy and fully cooked through. Halfway through the cooking time, remove the basket and turn the wings over to ensure they're cooking evenly.
8. When the wings are done, carefully remove them from the air fryer and place them in a serving dish.
9. Sprinkle with the chopped fresh coriander before serving.

NUTRITION FACTS PER 100G:
Energy: 220kcal | Protein: 18.5g | Total Fat: 15.2g | Saturated Fat: 3.7g | Carbohydrates: 4.6g | Sugars: 1.5g | Dietary Fibre: 0.7g

BRIE AND CRANBERRY PARCELS

Servings: 4 | Difficulty: Easy | Temperature: 200 degrees Celsius |
Preparation Time: 15 minutes | Cooking Time: 15-20 minutes

INGREDIENTS:

- 100g brie
- 4 tablespoons cranberry sauce
- puff pastry sheets, as needed
- 1 egg for egg wash

PREPARATION:

1. Preheat the air fryer to 200 degrees Celsius.
2. Roll out the puff pastry sheets on a floured surface until they are thin.
3. Cut the pastry sheets into 8 squares that are roughly the same size.
4. Cut the Brie into 4 slices and place a slice on each square of pastry.
5. Place a tablespoon of cranberry sauce on top of the Brie on each square of pastry.
6. Fold the corners of the pastry squares into the middle to form a parcel shape, ensuring all cheese and cranberry sauce are enclosed within.
7. Beat the egg in a bowl and lightly brush each parcel with the egg wash for a golden finish.
8. Place the parcels in the air fryer basket, making sure they don't touch each other.
9. Cook in the air fryer for about 15-20 minutes until they are golden-brown and crispy.
10. Leave the parcels to cool for a few minutes before serving as the cheese inside will be very hot. Be careful not to burn yourself!

NUTRITION FACTS PER 100G:
Energy: 300kcal | Protein: 10g | Total Fat: 20g | Saturated Fat: 8g |
Carbohydrates: 20g | Sugars: 10g | Dietary Fibre: 1g

SMOKED SALMON BLINIS

Servings: 2 | Difficulty: Medium | Temperature: 180 degrees Celsius |
Preparation Time: 40 minutes | Cooking Time: 10 minutes

INGREDIENTS:

- 50g buckwheat flour
- 25g plain flour
- 1/2 teaspoon baking powder
- 1 pinch of salt
- 125ml skimmed milk
- 1 small egg
- 60g smoked salmon
- 100g full-fat cream cheese
- 1 tablespoon chopped fresh chives
- 1 tablespoon rapeseed oil

PREPARATION:

1. Start by sifting the buckwheat flour, plain flour, baking powder, and the pinch of salt into a large mixing bowl.
2. In another smaller bowl, whisk together the skimmed milk and egg. Gradually add this to the flour mix and continue stirring until well combined. You should be left with a smooth batter.
3. Leave the mixture to rest for approximately 30 minutes, allowing the buckwheat to absorb the liquid.
4. Once the mixture has rested, preheat your air-fryer to 180 degrees Celsius.
5. Brush your air fryer with a thin layer of rapeseed oil to prevent sticking. Spoon small dollops of the batter onto the warm surface, cooking them in batches for around 5 minutes on each side or until the blinis are airy and cooked through.
6. Allow them to cool slightly and set aside.
7. In the meantime, cut smoked salmon into small neat strips or squares and set aside.
8. Spread a generous layer of cream cheese over each of the cooled blinis.
9. Top each blini with a small amount of the freshly cut smoked salmon.
10. Sprinkle freshly chopped chives on top to finish.

NUTRITION FACTS PER 100G:
Energy: 145kcal | Protein: 8g | Total Fat: 7g | Saturated Fat: 3g | Carbohydrates: 11g | Sugars: 2g | Dietary Fibre: 1g

STUFFED VINE LEAVES

Servings: 4 | Difficulty: Medium | Temperature: 180 degrees Celsius |
Preparation Time: 50 minutes | Cooking Time: 30 minutes

INGREDIENTS:

- 20 fresh vinc lcaves, or vine leaves from a jar
- 100g short-grain white rice
- 1 onion, finely chopped
- 2 cloves of garlic, minced
- 50g pine nuts
- 1 small handful fresh mint, finely chopped
- 1 small handful fresh flat-leaf parsley, finely chopped
- 1 tablespoon olive oil
- juice of 1 lemon
- salt and black pepper to taste
- 200ml vegetable stock

PREPARATION:

1. If using fresh vine leaves, wash them properly and blanch in boiling water for 2-3 minutes. If using leaves from a jar, just rinse and pat dry.
2. Rinse the rice under cold water until the water runs clear. Leave to drain.
3. In a frying pan, heat the olive oil and add the onions and garlic. Cook until soft.
4. Add the rice and pine nuts to the pan, and cook for about 5 minutes until the pine nuts start to brown.
5. Remove the pan from the heat and stir in the mint, parsley, and lemon juice. Season with salt and pepper and set aside to cool.
6. Once the rice mixture has cooled, take a vine leaf and put a small spoonful of the rice mixture onto the leaf. Fold in the sides and roll up tightly, continuing this process until all the mixture and vine leaves are used.
7. Arrange the stuffed vine leaves in a single layer in the air fryer basket.
8. Pour the vegetable stock over the vine leaves.
9. Air fry the vine leaves at 180 degrees Celsius for about 25-30 minutes until the leaves are cooked through and slightly crispy on the edges.
10. Remove the stuffed vine leaves carefully with tongs, and allow them to rest for a few minutes before serving.

NUTRITION FACTS PER 100G:
Energy: 150kcal | Protein: 3.5g | Total Fat: 5g | Saturated Fat: 0.7g |
Carbohydrates: 22g | Sugars: 2g | Dietary Fibre: 1.5g

TEMPURA VEGETABLES

Servings: 4 | Difficulty: Medium | Temperature: 200 degrees Celsius |
Preparation Time: 15 minutes | Cooking Time: 12 minutes

INGREDIENTS:

- 200g assorted vegetables (courgettes, carrots, aubergine, bell peppers)
- 100g plain flour
- 50g cornflour
- 1 teaspoon baking powder
- 250ml sparkling water, chilled
- salt to taste
- 2 tablespoons sesame oil

PREPARATION:

1. Start by washing all the vegetables, then slice them into bite-sized pieces, try to keep all the pieces roughly the same size.
2. In a large bowl, combine the plain flour, cornflour, and baking powder.
3. Gradually mix in the chilled sparkling water, whisking until you have a smooth batter.
4. Season the batter with salt according to your taste.
5. Heat up your air fryer to 200 degrees Celsius.
6. Dip each piece of vegetable into the batter, then place it in the air fryer basket. Do not overcrowd the basket.
7. Once the basket is filled, close the air fryer and set to cook for 12 minutes.
8. After 6 minutes, carefully flip each of the vegetable pieces to ensure they cook evenly.
9. Once the pieces are golden and crispy, they are ready to be served. Carefully remove them from the air fryer and drizzle with a little bit of sesame oil for a nutty flavour.
10. Continue with remaining vegetables until all are air-fried.

NUTRITION FACTS PER 100G:
Energy: 98kcal | Protein: 2.4g | Total Fat: 3.4g | Saturated Fat: 0.5g |
Carbohydrates: 14.5g | Sugars: 1.9g | Dietary Fibre: 1.2g.

POTTED SHRIMP CAKES

Servings: 4 | Difficulty: Medium | Temperature: 180 degrees Celsius |
Preparation Time: 45 minutes | Cooking Time: 15 minutes

INGREDIENTS:

- ✪ 200g cooked, peeled shrimps
- ✪ 150g mashed potatoes
- ✪ 3 tablespoons lemon juice
- ✪ 2 tablespoons fresh chopped parsley
- ✪ 1 tablespoon fresh chopped chives
- ✪ 50g melted unsalted butter
- ✪ 2 eggs
- ✪ 100g bread crumbs
- ✪ salt and pepper to taste
- ✪ 2 tablespoons olive oil for brushing

PREPARATION:

1. In a large bowl, mash the cooked, peeled shrimps into small chunks.
2. Add the mashed potatoes to the bowl with the shrimps.
3. Drizzle in the lemon juice and sprinkle in the fresh chopped parsley and chives.
4. Pour in the melted unsalted butter and mix all the ingredients together well.
5. Season with the salt and pepper to taste.
6. Form the mixture into small, thick cakes.
7. In a separate bowl, beat the eggs and set this aside.
8. Pour the breadcrumbs into a separate dish.
9. Dip each shrimp cake into the beaten eggs and then roll it in the breadcrumbs until fully covered.
10. Preheat the air fryer to 180 degrees Celsius.
11. Place the shrimp cakes into the air fryer basket, making sure they are not touching.
12. Brush each cake lightly with some olive oil.
13. Cook at 180 degrees Celsius for 15 minutes, or until golden brown and crispy.
14. Remove the shrimp cakes from the air fryer and serve immediately.

NUTRITION FACTS PER 100G:
Energy: 200kcal | Protein: 9g | Total Fat: 8g | Saturated Fat: 3g |
Carbohydrates: 18g | Sugars: 2g | Dietary Fibre: 1g

MELON AND PARMA HAM BITES

Servings: 6 | Difficulty: Easy | Temperature: 200 degrees Celsius | Preparation Time: 15 minutes | Cooking Time: 5 minutes

INGREDIENTS:

- 500g cantaloupe melon
- 200g Parma ham
- 100ml olive oil
- 2 tablespoons balsamic glaze
- a handful of fresh basil leaves
- salt and black pepper for seasoning
- bamboo skewers

PREPARATION:

1. Start by pre-heating your air fryer to 200 degrees Celsius.
2. Cut the cantaloupe melon into bite-sized pieces.
3. Lay a piece of Parma ham flat on a cutting board. Place a piece of melon at one end of the ham slice and roll up tightly.
4. Skewer the ham and melon roll onto a bamboo skewer. Continue this until all the melon pieces are rolled in Parma ham and skewered.
5. Now, place the skewered ham and melon bites in the basket of the air fryer.
6. Cook them in the preheated air fryer for about 5 minutes, or until the ham begins to be crispy.
7. While the bites are cooking, blend the olive oil and balsamic glaze together with a whisk in a bowl. Season this mixture with some salt and pepper.
8. Once ready, remove the bites from the air fryer and place them on a serving plate.
9. Drizzle the olive oil and balsamic glaze mixture over the bites.
10. To finish, sprinkle freshly chopped basil leaves over the melon and Parma ham bites.

NUTRITION FACTS PER 100G:
Energy: 78kcal | Protein: 3.8g | Total Fat: 2.6g | Saturated Fat: 0.8g | Carbohydrates: 5.8g | Sugars: 5.2g | Dietary Fibre: 0.7g

DEVILLED EGGS

Servings: 4 | Difficulty: Medium | Temperature: 200 degrees Celsius | Preparation Time: 25 minutes | Cooking Time: 17 minutes

INGREDIENTS:

- ✪ 6 large free range eggs
- ✪ 30g mayonnaise
- ✪ 15g dijon mustard
- ✪ 1 tablespoon white vinegar
- ✪ 1 teaspoon sea salt
- ✪ 1 teaspoon white pepper
- ✪ 1 teaspoon cayenne pepper or smoked paprika
- ✪ 1 tablespoon freshly chopped chives

PREPARATION:

1. Preheat the air fryer to 200 degrees Celsius.
2. Place the eggs in the air fryer basket carefully to avoid cracking.
3. Air fry the eggs for 15 minutes, then carefully shake the basket halfway through cooking.
4. Once done, immerse the eggs in a bowl of ice water for 10 minutes to cool and stop the cooking process.
5. After cooling, peel the shell off each egg and cut each egg in half lengthwise.
6. Scoop out the yolk using a small spoon and transfer yolks to a separate bowl.
7. Mash the yolks using a fork until crumbly.
8. Add the mayonnaise, Dijon mustard, vinegar, salt, white pepper to the mashed yolks and mix until smooth.
9. Pipe or spoon yolk mixture back into the whites of each egg half.
10. Sprinkle with Cayenne pepper or smoked paprika and freshly chopped chives.
11. Reheat in the air fryer for 2 minutes just before serving, ensuring the yokes are covered to prevent them from drying out. Serve, and enjoy your Devilled Eggs made for an Air Fryer!

NUTRITION FACTS PER 100G:
Energy: 154kcal | Protein: 10.2g | Total Fat: 11.5g | Saturated Fat: 3.2g | Carbohydrates: 2g | Sugars: 1g | Dietary Fibre: 0.2g

Chapter 3:
Fish and Poultry Selections (25 recipes)

COD AND CHIPS

Servings: 4 | Difficulty: Easy | Temperature: 200 degrees Celsius |
Preparation Time: 10 minutes | Cooking Time: 15-20 minutes

INGREDIENTS:

- 800g white potatoes, cut into chips
- 4 cod fillets, approx 150g each
- 2 tablespoons olive oil
- 1 tablespoon plain flour
- 1 tablespoon paprika
- salt and cracked black pepper to taste
- 1 tablespoon vinegar
- lemon wedges to serve

PREPARATION:

1. Preheat the air fryer to 200 degrees Celsius.
2. In a large bowl, toss the potato chips with 1 tablespoon olive oil, then season with salt and pepper.
3. Transfer the chips to the air fryer and cook for around 10 minutes, until they are nearly done but still a little firm in the centre.
4. While the chips are cooking, pat the cod fillets dry with a paper towel. In another bowl, mix the flour, paprika, and a sprinkle of salt and pepper.
5. Lightly brush each side of the cod fillets with the remaining tablespoon of olive oil, then dredge them through the flour mixture until they're covered.
6. Remove the chips from the air fryer and shake them up a bit so they cook evenly. Place the cod fillets on top of the chips.
7. Cook in the air fryer for another 5-10 minutes, until the fillets are crispy and golden, and the chips are cooked through.
8. Splash the vinegar over the chips, and serve immediately with lemon wedges on the side.

NUTRITION FACTS PER 100G:
Energy: 115kcal | Protein: 10.2g | Total Fat: 3.5g | Saturated Fat: 0.5g |
Carbohydrates: 10.0g | Sugars: 0.8g | Dietary Fibre: 1.2g

LEMON AND HERB CHICKEN THIGHS

Servings: 4 | Difficulty: Medium | Temperature: 190 degrees Celsius |
Preparation Time: 25 minutes | Cooking Time: 20 minutes

INGREDIENTS:

- 8 bone-in, skin-on chicken thighs (approximately 1kg)
- zest and juice of 2 lemons
- 4 tablespoons olive oil
- 4 cloves of garlic, minced
- 2 tablespoons finely chopped fresh rosemary
- 2 tablespoons finely chopped fresh thyme
- 1 tablespoon finely chopped fresh parsley
- salt and black pepper to taste

PREPARATION:

1. Rinse the chicken thighs under cold running water, then pat dry using kitchen paper. Set aside.
2. In a large bowl, combine the lemon zest, lemon juice, olive oil, minced garlic, rosemary, thyme, and parsley. Stir well to combine.
3. Season the mixture with salt and black pepper, then place the chicken thighs in the bowl. Toss to coat all the chicken pieces evenly.
4. Cover the bowl and refrigerate for at least 15 minutes to allow the chicken to marinate.
5. Preheat your air fryer to 190 degrees Celsius.
6. Remove the chicken thighs from the bowl, allowing any excess marinade to drop off.
7. Place the chicken thighs, skin-side up, in the air fryer basket, ensuring not to overcrowd them. You may need to cook them in batches depending on the size of your air fryer.
8. Cook for 10 minutes, then flip the thighs over and cook for another 10 minutes or until the chicken is cooked through and the skin is crispy.
9. Allow the chicken thighs to rest for a few minutes before serving.

NUTRITION FACTS PER 100G:
Energy: 220kcal | Protein: 15g | Total Fat: 16g | Saturated Fat: 4g |
Carbohydrates: 2g | Sugars: 1g | Dietary Fibre: 0.5g

PIRI PIRI CHICKEN DRUMSTICKS

Servings: 4 | Difficulty: Medium | Temperature: 200 degrees Celsius |
Preparation Time: 40 minutes | Cooking Time: 25 minutes

INGREDIENTS:

- ✪ 8 chicken drumsticks
- ✪ 2 tablespoons olive oil
- ✪ 2 cloves of garlic, minced
- ✪ 1 tablespoon paprika
- ✪ 2 tablespoons Piri Piri seasoning
- ✪ juice of 1 lemon
- ✪ 30g fresh coriander, finely chopped
- ✪ 1 red chilli, deseeded and finely chopped
- ✪ salt, to taste
- ✪ 1 tablespoon honey

PREPARATION:

1. Wash the chicken drumsticks and pat dry using a paper towel.
2. In a bowl, mix the olive oil, minced garlic, paprika, Piri Piri seasoning, lemon juice, chopped coriander, chopped chilli, salt, and honey.
3. Add the chicken drumsticks to this marinade. Coat the chicken pieces thoroughly with this mixture. Let the chicken marinade for about 30 minutes.
4. Preheat your air fryer to 200 degrees Celsius.
5. Arrange the marinated drumsticks in the air fryer basket leaving a bit of space between each drumstick.
6. Cook the chicken drumsticks at 200 degrees Celsius for about 25 minutes. Make sure to turn the drumsticks halfway through the cooking time to ensure they cook evenly.
7. Check that the drumsticks are fully cooked by inserting a skewer – the juices should run clear. If they're not quite there, cook for a further 5-7 minutes and check again.
8. Once cooked, remove the drumsticks from the air fryer and let them rest for a few minutes before serving.

NUTRITION FACTS PER 100G:
Energy: 190kcal | Protein: 23g | Total Fat: 9g | Saturated Fat: 2g |
Carbohydrates: 4g | Sugars: 1g | Dietary Fibre: 0.5g

SMOKED HADDOCK GRATIN

Servings: 4 | Difficulty: Medium | Temperature: 180 degrees Celsius |
Preparation Time: 15 minutes | Cooking Time: 20 minutes

INGREDIENTS:

- 500g smoked haddock fillets
- 500ml milk
- 1 bay leaf
- 1 small onion, finely chopped
- 2 cloves garlic, minced
- 1 tablespoon olive oil
- 75g plain flour
- 50g unsalted butter
- 100g mature cheddar cheese, grated
- 2 tablespoons fresh parsley, chopped
- salt and black pepper to taste

PREPARATION:

1. Start by placing the haddock in a large, shallow pan, covering it with the milk, and adding the bay leaf.
2. Gently bring to the boil on a medium heat, then reduce the heat and let it simmer for 8-10 minutes.
3. Carefully remove the haddock from the milk and set aside, keeping the milk.
4. In a different pan, heat the olive oil over medium heat and sauté the onion and garlic until they're softened.
5. Melt the butter in a separate saucepan, then slowly stir in the flour to form a roux.
6. Gradually add the milk you kept earlier, stirring continuously to ensure the mixture stays smooth.
7. Bring the mixture to the boil, then reduce the heat and cook for a further 2 minutes.
8. Stir in 3/4 of the cheddar cheese, the cooked onion and garlic, and the parsley. Season with salt and pepper to taste, then remove from the heat.
9. Flake the haddock into chunks and fold into the cheese sauce.
10. Spoon the haddock and sauce mixture into 4gratin dishes or a large foil tray that fits into your air fryer basket.
11. Sprinkle with the remaining cheddar cheese.
12. Place the gratin dishes or foil tray into the air fryer and cook at 180 degrees Celsius for 20 minutes, or until the top is a golden brown and bubbling.

NUTRITION FACTS PER 100G:
Energy: 112kcal | Protein: 10.1g | Total Fat: 5.8g | Saturated Fat: 2.9g |
Carbohydrates: 4.8g | Sugars: 2.4g | Dietary Fibre: 0.2g

THAI SPICED DUCK LEGS

Servings: 4 | Difficulty: Medium | Temperature: 190 degrees Celsius |
Preparation Time: 15 minutes | Cooking Time: 30 minutes

INGREDIENTS:

- ✪ 4 duck legs (approximately 400g each)
- ✪ 2 teaspoons of coriander seeds
- ✪ 1 teaspoon of cumin seeds
- ✪ 4 cloves of garlic, minced
- ✪ 1 tablespoon of grated fresh root ginger
- ✪ 2 red chillies, deseeded and finely chopped
- ✪ 4 tablespoons of fish sauce
- ✪ 4 tablespoons of light soy sauce
- ✪ zest and juice of 2 limes
- ✪ 2 tablespoons of vegetable oil

PREPARATION:

1. Begin by toasting the coriander and cumin seeds in a dry frying pan over medium heat until they become fragrant. This should take no more than a few minutes.
2. Transfer the toasted seeds to a pestle and mortar and grind them up until they become a fine powder.
3. In a large bowl, combine the ground coriander and cumin with the minced garlic, grated ginger, chopped chillies, fish sauce, soy sauce and the zest and juice of your limes.
4. Add the duck legs to the large bowl and turn them in the mixture until they are thoroughly coated. If time permits, let them marinate in the fridge for a few hours or overnight.
5. Preheat your air fryer to 190 degrees Celsius.
6. Carefully place the marinated duck legs in the air fryer. Be cautious not to overcrowd the air fryer, you may need to cook in batches depending on the size of your air fryer.
7. Cook the duck legs for approximately 30 minutes or until they are golden brown and cooked through, turning them halfway through the cooking time.
8. Once done, let the duck legs rest for a few minutes before serving. This ensures the juices redistribute, resulting in succulent and flavoursome meat.

NUTRITION FACTS PER 100G:
Energy: 224kcal | Protein: 17g | Total Fat: 15g | Saturated Fat: 4g |
Carbohydrates: 7g | Sugars: 3g | Dietary Fibre: 1g

TANDOORI CHICKEN SKEWERS

Servings: 4 | Difficulty: Medium | Temperature: 200 degrees Celsius |
Preparation Time: 2 hours (including marinating time) | Cooking Time: 15 minutes

INGREDIENTS:

- 500g of boneless chicken breast
- juice of 1 lemon
- 150g of plain yoghurt
- 2 tablespoons of vegetable or sunflower oil
- 2 tablespoons of Tandoori masala
- 1 tablespoon of coriander powder
- 1 tablespoon of cumin powder
- pinch of salt
- 2 cloves of garlic, finely crushed
- 1 inch of fresh ginger, finely grated
- 1 large white onion, finely chopped
- wooden skewers (soaked in water for 30 minutes)

PREPARATION:

1. Rinse the chicken breast and cut them into 2-inch size pieces.
2. In a bowl, combine lemon juice, plain yoghurt, oil, Tandoori masala, coriander powder, cumin powder, salt, crushed garlic, and grated ginger to form a marinade.
3. Add the chicken pieces to the marinade, making sure each piece is well coated. Cover the bowl and let it marinade in the fridge for a minimum of 2 hours or overnight if time allows.
4. Remove the marinated chicken from the fridge and thread onto soaked skewers, interspersed with chopped onions.
5. Preheat the air fryer at 200 degrees Celsius.
6. Place the skewers in the air fryer basket, ensuring they are not touching each other.
7. Air fry for approximately 15 minutes, turning the skewers halfway through, until the chicken is thoroughly cooked and slightly charred on the edges.
8. Once done, remove the skewers from the air fryer and let them rest for a few minutes before serving.

NUTRITION FACTS PER 100G:
Energy: 150kcal | Protein: 18g | Total Fat: 8g | Saturated Fat: 1g |
Carbohydrates: 2g | Sugars: 1g | Dietary Fibre: 0.6g

SEA BASS WITH MEDITERRANEAN SALSA

Servings: 4 | Difficulty: Medium | Temperature: 200 degrees Celsius |
Preparation Time: 20 minutes | Cooking Time: 15 minutes

INGREDIENTS:

- 4 sea bass fillets, 150g each
- 2 tablespoons extra virgin olive oil
- salt and pepper to taste
- 150g cherry tomatoes, halved
- 100g black olives, pitted and chopped
- 50g capers, rinsed
- 1 red onion, finely chopped
- 1 garlic clove, minced
- zest and juice of 1 lemon
- 2 tablespoons fresh parsley, finely chopped
- 1 teaspoon dried oregano

PREPARATION:

1. Preheat your air fryer to 200 degrees Celsius.
2. Rinse the sea bass fillets under cold water and pat dry with kitchen paper. Drizzle 1 tablespoon of olive oil over the fillets. Season with salt and pepper. Set aside.
3. In a bowl, combine cherry tomatoes, black olives, capers, red onion, garlic, lemon zest, lemon juice, parsley, oregano and the remaining olive oil. Stir well to combine.
4. Place the sea bass fillets into the air fryer basket, ensuring they are not overlapping. Cook for 10 minutes.
5. After 10 minutes, carefully pull out the basket and top each fillet with an even portion of the Mediterranean salsa.
6. Return the basket to the air fryer and continue cooking for another 5 minutes or until the fish is flaky and cooked through.
7. Carefully remove the fish from the air fryer. Serve hot with extra Mediterranean salsa on the side if desired.

NUTRITION FACTS PER 100G:
Energy: 140kcal | Protein: 16g | Total Fat: 7g | Saturated Fat: 1.5g |
Carbohydrates: 4g | Sugar: 1.3g | Dietary Fibre: 1g

HERB-CRUSTED TURKEY STEAKS

Servings: 4 | Difficulty: Medium | Temperature: 180 degrees Celsius |
Preparation Time: 15 minutes | Cooking Time: 20 minutes

INGREDIENTS:

- 4 turkey steaks (approx. 150g each)
- 2 tablespoons olive oil
- 1/2 teaspoon garlic granules
- 1/2 teaspoon onion granules
- 1 tablespoon dried mixed herbs (parsley, thyme, rosemary, oregano)
- salt and freshly ground black pepper
- 1 tablespoon dijon mustard
- 100g breadcrumbs

PREPARATION:

1. Preheat the air fryer to 180 degrees Celsius.
2. Trim any excess fat off the turkey steaks and pat them dry.
3. In a bowl, combine the garlic granules, onion granules, mixed herbs, salt, and freshly ground black pepper. This will form your herb mixture for crusting.
4. Brush each turkey steak lightly with olive oil, ensuring each steak is evenly coated.
5. Apply a light coat of dijon mustard over each steak. This will help the herb mixture adhere to the steaks.
6. Press each side of the turkey steaks into the herb mixture. They should be fully coated.
7. Nuance the breadcrumbs onto the herb-coated turkey steaks. Ensure they are adequately covered.
8. Place the steaks into the air fryer basket, ensuring they do not overlap.
9. Cook the turkey steaks for 10 minutes, then turn them over. Cook for another 10 minutes or until the outside is crispy and golden-brown, and the inside is no longer pink.
10. Serve the herb-crusted turkey steaks with your favourite accompaniments.

NUTRITION FACTS PER 100G:
Energy: 135kcal | Protein: 17.2g | Total Fat: 4.8g | Saturated Fat: 1.2g |
Carbohydrates: 5.5g | Sugars: 0.8g | Dietary Fibre: 0.7g

AIR-FRIED CHICKEN KIEV

Servings: 4 | Difficulty: Medium | Temperature: 180 degrees Celsius |
Preparation Time: 60 minutes | Cooking Time: 25 minutes

INGREDIENTS:

- 4 chicken breasts (approximately 200g each)
- 100g unsalted butter, softened
- 2 garlic cloves, finely minced
- 4 tablespoons chopped fresh parsley
- 100g plain flour
- 2 large eggs
- 200g breadcrumbs
- 2 tablespoons vegetable oil
- salt and pepper to taste

PREPARATION:

1. Mix the butter, minced garlic, and parsley in a bowl until well combined. Season with salt and pepper to taste.
2. Using a sharp knife, make a pocket in the thickest part of each chicken breast, being careful not to cut all the way through.
3. Fill the pockets with the garlic butter mixture, then press the edges of the chicken together to seal.
4. Put the flour, eggs, and breadcrumbs in three separate shallow dishes.
5. Season each chicken breast with salt and pepper, then dredge in the flour, dip into the eggs, and coat in the breadcrumbs, ensuring it is fully covered. Repeat these steps for each chicken breast.
6. Place the coated chicken breasts in the fridge for at least 30 minutes. This will help the coating stick to the chicken during cooking.
7. Preheat your air fryer to 180 degrees Celsius.
8. Brush the chicken breasts with the vegetable oil, then place them in the air fryer basket, leaving enough space between each piece so they don't touch.
9. Cook for 25 minutes or until the chicken is golden brown and cooked through.
10. Let the chicken rest for a few minutes before serving to allow the juices to redistribute.

NUTRITION FACTS PER 100G:
Energy: 220kcal | Protein: 18.6g | Total Fat: 13.2g | Saturated Fat: 5.7g |
Carbohydrates: 8.9g | Sugars: 0.9g | Dietary Fibre: 0.6g

PAELLA-STYLE SEAFOOD MIX

Servings: 4 | Difficulty: Medium | Temperature: 200 degrees Celsius |
Preparation Time: 15 minutes | Cooking Time: 25 minutes

INGREDIENTS:

- 300g mixed seafood (prawns, mussels, and squid)
- 2 tablespoons olive oil
- 120g paella rice
- 1 onion, finely chopped
- 1 red bell pepper, chopped
- 2 garlic cloves, minced
- 1 teaspoon paprika
- 1 teaspoon turmeric
- 200ml vegetable stock
- 1 small can chopped tomatoes
- salt and pepper to taste
- 2 tablespoons fresh parsley, chopped
- 1 lemon, cut into wedges

PREPARATION:

1. Put the air fryer to preheat at 200 degrees Celsius.
2. Rinse the seafood under cold water, pat dry, and set aside.
3. In a large bowl, combine the paella rice with the olive oil, onion, red pepper, garlic, paprika, turmeric, and a pinch of salt and pepper. Stir to combine and coat the rice and vegetables with the spices and oil.
4. Transfer the mixture to the air fryer basket. Make sure it is spread evenly in a single layer.
5. Cook in the preheated air fryer for 10 minutes, shaking the basket halfway through to ensure even cooking.
6. After the initial 10 minutes, add the seafood, chopped tomatoes, and vegetable stock to the air fryer basket. Stir gently to combine.
7. Continue to cook in the air fryer for another 15 minutes, or until the seafood is cooked through and the rice is tender.
8. Sprinkle the cooked paella with the fresh parsley and serve with lemon wedges. Season with extra salt and pepper if necessary.

NUTRITION FACTS PER 100G:
Energy: 109kcal | Protein: 6.7g | Total Fat: 3.8g | Saturated Fat: 0.6g |
Carbohydrates: 11.5g | Sugars: 2g | Dietary Fibre: 1.4g

PRAWN AND CHORIZO JAMBALAYA

Servings: 4 | Difficulty: Medium | Temperature: 180 degrees Celsius |
Preparation Time: 15 minutes | Cooking Time: 20 minutes

INGREDIENTS:

- 400g of prawns, peeled and deveined
- 200g chorizo, thinly sliced
- 200g long grain rice, rinsed
- 150g red and green bell pepper, diced
- 1 onion, diced
- 2 cloves of garlic, minced
- 1 teaspoon smoked paprika
- 1 teaspoon dried thyme
- 1/2 teaspoon cayenne pepper
- 800ml chicken stock
- 200g canned peeled tomatoes
- 2 tablespoons olive oil
- salt, to taste
- freshly ground black pepper, to taste
- 2 tablespoons chopped fresh parsley for garnish

PREPARATION:

1. Preheat your air fryer to 180 degrees Celsius.
2. In a pan over medium heat, add the olive oil, diced onion, diced bell peppers, and garlic. Cook until the onions are translucent and the peppers are soft.
3. Add the sliced chorizo to the pan and cook until it begins to crisp.
4. Stir in the prawns, making sure they are evenly distributed amongst the chorizo. Cook for about 3 minutes, or until the prawns start to turn pink.
5. Sprinkle over the smoked paprika, dried thyme, cayenne pepper, salt, and black pepper. Stir well to ensure all the ingredients are well coated in the spices.
6. Add the rice to the pan and stir until the grains are coated in the oils and spices.
7. Add the peeled tomatoes and chicken stock to the pan, stir well, and bring the mixture to a light simmer.
8. Transfer the jambalaya mixture to a baking dish that fits in your air fryer.
9. Cook in the air fryer for 20 minutes, shaking the basket after 10 minutes, until the rice is tender and has absorbed most of the liquid.
10. Garnish with fresh chopped parsley before serving.

NUTRITION FACTS PER 100G:
Energy: 150kcal | Protein: 9g | Total Fat: 7g | Saturated Fat: 2g |
Carbohydrates: 12g | Sugars: 1g | Dietary Fibre: 1g

CHICKEN AND MUSHROOM PIE

Servings: 6 | Difficulty: Medium | Temperature: 180 degrees Celsius |
Preparation Time: 25 minutes | Cooking Time: 25 minutes

INGREDIENTS:

- 500g boneless chicken breast, chopped into small pieces
- 200g button mushrooms, sliced
- 2 medium-sized onions, diced
- 4 garlic cloves, minced
- 2 tablespoons sunflower oil
- 1 teaspoon dried thyme
- 500ml chicken stock
- 200ml double cream
- 2 tablespoons self-raising flour
- salt and pepper to taste
- 1 packet of frozen puff pastry, defrosted
- 1 beaten egg for glazing

PREPARATION:

1. Preheat your air fryer to 180 degrees Celsius.
2. In a large frying pan, heat up 1 tablespoon of sunflower oil over medium heat and sauté the onions and garlic until they are transparent.
3. In the same pan, add the chicken and cook it until it is thoroughly cooked and no pink parts are visible.
4. Remove the chicken, onions and garlic from the pan and set aside leaving the oil in the pan.
5. Add the mushrooms to the pan and cook them until they soften.
6. Once the mushrooms are done, add the chicken, onions and garlic back into the frying pan. Sprinkle the flour over the mix and stir well to combine everything. Cook for a couple of minutes.
7. Pour in the chicken stock, double cream, and dried thyme. Stir everything together, season with salt and pepper, and allow the mixture to simmer for about 10 minutes until the sauce has thickened.
8. While the mixture is simmering, roll out the puff pastry using a little flour to prevent it from sticking.
9. Once the chicken mixture is done simmering, transfer it to a pie dish. Cover the pie dish with the rolled-out puff pastry, tucking in the edges.
10. Brush the top of the pastry with the beaten egg for glazing.

11. Using a sharp knife, make a small slit in the centre of the pastry to allow steam to escape during cooking.
12. Carefully transfer the pie into the preheated air fryer and cook for 25 minutes, or until the pastry is golden brown.
13. Let the pie cool for a couple of minutes before serving.

NUTRITION FACTS PER 100G:
Energy: 220kcal | Protein: 14g | Total Fat: 12g | Saturated Fat: 4g | Carbohydrates: 15g | Sugars: 2g | Dietary Fibre: 0.5g

LEMON SOLE GOUJONS

Servings: 4 | Difficulty: Easy | Temperature: 180 degrees Celsius |
Preparation Time: 20 minutes | Cooking Time: 10 minutes

INGREDIENTS:

- 450g fillets of lemon sole
- 80g flour
- 1 teaspoon salt
- 1 teaspoon ground black pepper
- 2 medium eggs
- 170g breadcrumbs
- zest of 1 lemon
- 2 tablespoons sunflower oil
- lemon wedges
- 1 tablespoon chopped fresh parsley

PREPARATION:

1. Cut the lemon sole fillets into goujon-sized pieces.
2. In a bowl, mix the flour, salt, and black pepper together.
3. In a separate bowl, beat the eggs.
4. In a third bowl, mix the breadcrumbs with the lemon zest.
5. Dredge each piece of fish first in the flour mixture, then dip in the beaten egg, making sure to coat it completely.
6. Roll the egg-coated fish piece in the breadcrumb mixture until it is completely covered. Repeat this process for all of the fish pieces.
7. Place the prepared fish pieces in the air fryer basket after brushing each one with sunflower oil.
8. Set the air fryer to 180 degrees Celsius and cook for 10 minutes.
9. Shake the air fryer basket halfway through to ensure the fish cook evenly.
10. Serve the Lemon Sole Goujons garnished with lemon wedges and chopped parsley.

NUTRITION FACTS PER 100G:
Energy: 150kcal | Protein: 15g | Total Fat: 8g | Saturated Fat: 1.5g |
Carbohydrates: 7g | Sugars: 0.5g | Dietary Fibre: 0.5g

CHICKEN CAESAR SALAD CUPS

Servings: 4 | Difficulty: Medium | Temperature: 190 degrees Celsius |
Preparation Time: 20 minutes | Cooking Time: 10 minutes

INGREDIENTS:

- ✪ 4 boneless chicken breasts (125g each)
- ✪ salt and pepper to taste
- ✪ 1 tablespoon olive oil
- ✪ 16 romaine lettuce leaves
- ✪ 100g parmesan cheese (shaved)
- ✪ 1 lemon (juiced)
- ✪ 2 cloves garlic (minced)
- ✪ 3 tablespoons mayonnaise
- ✪ 1 tablespoon Worcestershire sauce
- ✪ 2 tablespoons white wine vinegar
- ✪ 1 teaspoon dijon mustard
- ✪ 1 tablespoon anchovy paste
- ✪ 25g croutons (crushed)

PREPARATION:

1. Preheat the air fryer to 190 degrees Celsius.
2. Season the chicken breasts with salt and pepper, then brush them with olive oil.
3. Place the chicken breasts in the air fryer basket and cook for 10 minutes or until they reach an internal temperature of 74 degrees Celsius.
4. While the chicken is cooking, prepare the Caesar dressing. In a bowl, mix together the lemon juice, garlic, mayonnaise, Worcestershire sauce, white wine vinegar, Dijon mustard, and the anchovy paste.
5. Once the chicken is cooked, remove from the air fryer and let it cool. Then, slice it into thin strips.
6. To assemble the salad cups, place a few slices of chicken into each lettuce leaf, drizzle with the Caesar dressing, and top with shaved Parmesan and crushed croutons.
7. Serve immediately and enjoy the refreshing and light Chicken Caesar Salad Cups prepared using an air fryer.

NUTRITION FACTS PER 100G:
Energy: 209kcal | Protein: 22.2g | Total Fat: 11.4g | Saturated Fat: 3.1g | Carbohydrates: 3.1g | Sugars: 1.2g | Dietary Fibre: 0.7g

MOROCCAN CHICKEN AND APRICOT BAKE

Servings: 4 | Difficulty: Medium | Temperature: 180 degrees Celsius |
Preparation Time: 20 minutes | Cooking Time: 25 minutes

INGREDIENTS:

- 600g boneless chicken thighs
- 3 tablespoons olive oil
- 1 tablespoon Ras el-Hanout (Moroccan spice blend)
- zest and juice of one lemon
- 150g dried apricots
- 2 red onions, chopped
- 2 garlic cloves, finely chopped
- 400g tin of chickpeas, rinsed and drained
- 250ml chicken stock
- a handful of fresh coriander leaves, chopped
- salt and pepper to taste

PREPARATION:

1. Preheat your air fryer to 180 degrees Celsius.
2. Cut the chicken thighs into bite-sized pieces, season with salt and pepper.
3. In a bowl, mix 2 tablespoons of olive oil with the Ras el-Hanout, lemon zest, lemon juice. Add the chicken pieces to the bowl and ensure all the pieces are well coated with the mixture.
4. Place the chicken in the preheated air fryer and cook for 10 minutes, flipping halfway through.
5. While the chicken is cooking, heat the remaining tablespoon of olive oil in a pan. Sauté the chopped red onions for approximately 5 minutes until it starts to soften.
6. Add the garlic and dried apricots to the pan and continue to cook for an additional 2 minutes.
7. Stir in the chickpeas to the pan, then pour in the chicken stock. Allow the mix to simmer for a few minutes.
8. Once the chicken is cooked and golden brown, transfer it to the pan with the simmering mixture.
9. Toss everything together in the pan, ensuring the chicken is well immersed in the chickpeas and apricot mix.
10. Cook for an extra 10 minutes until everything is well combined and the sauce has slightly thickened.
11. Sprinkle the dish with fresh coriander before serving. The Moroccan Chicken and Apricot Bake is now ready to be enjoyed.

NUTRITION FACTS PER 100G:
Energy: 220kcal | Protein: 20g | Total Fat: 12g | Saturated Fat: 3g |
Carbohydrates: 13g | Sugars: 7g | Dietary Fibre: 2g

SPICED MACKEREL FILLETS

Servings: 4 | Difficulty: Medium | Temperature: 200 degrees Celsius |
Preparation Time: 10 minutes | Cooking Time: 15 minutes

INGREDIENTS:

- 4 mackerel fillets (approximately 550g total)
- 2 tablespoons olive oil
- 2 tablespoons lemon juice
- 1 tablespoon ground cumin
- 1 tablespoon ground turmeric
- 1 tablespoon ground coriander
- 1 teaspoon salt
- 1 teaspoon pepper
- 1 tablespoon fresh parsley, chopped (for garnish)

PREPARATION:

1. Preheat your air fryer to 200 degrees Celsius.
2. Rinse the mackerel fillets under cold water and pat dry with a paper towel.
3. In a small bowl, combine the olive oil, lemon juice, ground cumin, ground turmeric, ground coriander, salt and pepper. Mix until a smooth marinade forms.
4. Rub the marinade evenly over each mackerel fillet, ensuring to cover both sides. Let the fillets sit for 5 minutes to absorb the flavours.
5. Place the marinated mackerel fillets into the air fryer basket, making sure they are not overlapping.
6. Cook in the air fryer for 7-8 minutes, then flip the mackerel fillets and cook for another 7-8 minutes, until the fillets are golden and crisped to your liking.
7. Carefully remove the mackerel fillets from the air fryer.
8. Sprinkle the cooked fillets with fresh chopped parsley for garnish before serving.

NUTRITION FACTS PER 100G:
Energy: 155kcal | Protein: 20g | Total Fat: 7g | Saturated Fat: 1.6g |
Carbohydrates: 0.6g | Sugars: 0.4g | Dietary Fibre: 0.2g

BBQ PULLED CHICKEN

Servings: 6 | Difficulty: Easy | Temperature: 180 degrees Celsius |
Preparation Time: 25 minutes | Cooking Time: 20 minutes

INGREDIENTS:

- 1.8kg boneless, skinless chicken thighs
- 240ml BBQ sauce
- salt to taste
- pepper to taste
- 1 tablespoon vegetable oil
- 60ml apple cider vinegar
- 200g brown sugar
- 1 tablespoon Worcestershire sauce
- 1 tablespoon paprika
- 2 cloves garlic, minced
- 1 onion, finely chopped

PREPARATION:

1. Lightly season the chicken thighs with salt and pepper.
2. Place the seasoned chicken thighs in the air fryer basket. Ensure that they are not overlapping to allow even cooking.
3. Cook the thighs in the air fryer at 180 degrees Celsius for 20 minutes.
4. While the chicken is cooking, prepare the BBQ sauce: heat the vegetable oil in a saucepan over a medium heat.
5. Add the minced garlic and chopped onion to the oil, sauté until the onions are translucent.
6. Add the brown sugar, paprika, Worcestershire sauce, vinegar, BBQ sauce to the saucepan. Stir well to combine all the ingredients.
7. Simmer the mixture on low heat for 15 minutes, stirring occasionally, then remove from the heat.
8. Once the chicken is cooked, use a meat thermometer to verify it has reached an internal temperature of 74 degrees Celsius.
9. Let the cooked chicken cool slightly then use two forks to shred the meat into small, thin strips.
10. Add the shredded chicken to the saucepan with the BBQ sauce. Toss until all the chicken is evenly coated.
11. Return the coated chicken to the air fryer. Cook at 180 degrees Celsius for an additional 5 minutes to allow the sauce to caramelise slightly.
12. Once done, serve the BBQ pulled chicken hot, topped with additional BBQ sauce if desired.

NUTRITION FACTS PER 100G:
Energy: 225kcal | Protein: 15g | Total Fat: 10g | Saturated Fat: 2.5g |
Carbohydrates: 15g | Sugars: 12g | Dietary Fibre: 0.4g

CRISPY CHICKEN SCHNITZEL

Servings: 4 | Difficulty: Medium | Temperature: 180 degrees Celsius |
Preparation Time: 15 minutes | Cooking Time: 12 minutes

INGREDIENTS:

- ✪ 500g boneless chicken breasts, thinly sliced
- ✪ 1 teaspoon salt
- ✪ 1 teaspoon black pepper
- ✪ 2 tablespoons sunflower oil
- ✪ 100g flour
- ✪ 2 large eggs
- ✪ 200g breadcrumbs
- ✪ lemon wedges for service

PREPARATION:

1. Begin by seasoning the thinly sliced chicken breasts with salt and pepper on both sides.
2. Put the flour in one shallow dish, beat the eggs in another and spread out the breadcrumbs in a third one.
3. Dip the chicken in the flour, dusting off any excess, then dip into the beaten eggs and finally into the breadcrumbs. Make sure the chicken is fully coated.
4. Preheat the air fryer at 180 degrees Celsius for about 5 minutes.
5. Season the breaded chicken with a bit of sunflower oil and arrange them in a single layer in the air fryer basket.
6. Fry the schnitzel for around 6 minutes on each side or until the chicken is cooked through and the coating is crispy.
7. Allow them to sit for a minute or two after cooking to allow the juices to redistribute.
8. Before serving, squeeze over some lemon juice if desired.
9. Your Crispy Chicken Schnitzel is ready to be served alongside a preferred side dish, like chips or salad.

NUTRITION FACTS PER 100G:
Energy: 225kcal | Protein: 23g | Total Fat: 9.6g | Saturated Fat: 2.1g |
Carbohydrates: 14g | Sugars: 1g | Dietary Fibre: 1g

ASIAN-STYLE SEA BREAM

Servings: 4 | Difficulty: Medium | Temperature: 200 degrees Celsius |
Preparation Time: 20 minutes | Cooking Time: 15 minutes

INGREDIENTS:

- 2 whole sea bream fish, cleaned and gutted (around 500g each)
- 2 tablespoons light soy sauce
- 2 tablespoons sweet chilli sauce
- 2 tablespoons rice vinegar
- 4 tablespoons sesame oil
- 4 cloves of garlic, crushed
- 30g fresh ginger, grated
- 1 red chilli, sliced
- bunch of spring onions, chopped
- 4 lime wedges
- salt and pepper for seasoning
- 2 teaspoons sesame seeds for garnishing

PREPARATION:

1. Start by scoring the fish on its side with 3-4 cuts to allow more flavour to penetrate.
2. In a bowl, combine the soy sauce, sweet chilli sauce, rice vinegar, sesame oil, crushed garlic, grated ginger, and red chilli slices. Mix them well.
3. Marinate the scored sea bream in this mixture for at least 15 minutes.
4. Preheat the air fryer to 200 degrees Celsius.
5. Season the marinated fish with salt and pepper and place it into the preheated air-fryer.
6. Allow it to cook for around 15 minutes, or until the skin is crisp and the fish flakes easily when tested with a fork.
7. Sprinkle the cooked fish with the chopped spring onions and sesame seeds.
8. Serve the Asian-Style Sea Bream hot, with a lime wedge on the side for squeezing over.

NUTRITION FACTS PER 100G:
Energy: 139kcal | Protein: 19.5g | Total Fat: 4.8g | Saturated Fat: 1.3g |
Carbohydrates: 4g | Sugars: 1.4g | Dietary Fibre: 0.5g

JERK CHICKEN WINGS

Servings: 4 | Difficulty: Medium | Temperature: 180 degrees Celsius |
Preparation Time: 20 minutes | Cooking Time: 15-20 minutes

INGREDIENTS:

- 1kg chicken wings
- 50ml jerk sauce
- 3 tablespoons soya sauce
- 2 tablespoons brown sugar
- 1 tablespoon allspice
- 1 tablespoon thyme
- 2 garlic cloves, minced
- 2 tablespoons ginger, minced
- 1 tablespoon ground black pepper
- salt to taste
- 2 fresh green chillies, minced

PREPARATION:

1. Rinse chicken wings under cold water and pat dry with paper towels.
2. In a large bowl, combine jerk sauce, soya sauce, brown sugar, allspice, thyme, minced garlic, minced ginger, pepper, salt, and minced chillies. Stir well until the mixture is thoroughly combined.
3. Place chicken wings in the marinade, ensuring each piece is fully covered. Leave to marinate for at least 15 minutes, but ideally overnight in the refrigerator for best results.
4. Preheat the air fryer to 180 degrees Celsius.
5. Arrange the marinated chicken wings in the air fryer. Make sure not to overcrowd - depending on the size of your air fryer, you may need to cook in batches.
6. Cook for 15-20 minutes, or until the chicken wings are well caramelised and cooked through. Halfway through the cooking time, turn the wings to ensure they cook evenly.
7. Once cooked, remove the wings from the air fryer and let them rest for a few minutes before serving.

NUTRITION FACTS PER 100G:
Energy: 232kcal | Protein: 24g | Total Fat: 14g | Saturated Fat: 4g |
Carbohydrates: 3g | Sugars: 2g | Dietary Fibre: 0.5g

TERIYAKI SALMON SKEWERS

Servings: 4 | Difficulty: Medium | Temperature: 180 degrees Celsius |
Preparation Time: 35 minutes | Cooking Time: 10-12 minutes

INGREDIENTS:

- ✪ 4 salmon filets, cut into 2.5cm cubes (500g)
- ✪ 3 red peppers, cut into 2.5cm squares
- ✪ 2 courgettes, cut into 1cm rounds
- ✪ 1 pineapple, cut into 2.5cm cubes
- ✪ 240ml Teriyaki sauce
- ✪ 2 tablespoons sesame oil
- ✪ 2 tablespoons freshly squeezed lemon juice
- ✪ 1 tablespoon brown sugar
- ✪ 1 tablespoon freshly grated ginger
- ✪ 2 garlic cloves, minced
- ✪ 1 tablespoon cornflour
- ✪ 2 tablespoons water
- ✪ salt to taste
- ✪ pepper to taste

PREPARATION:

1. Begin by preparing your skewers. If using wooden skewers, pre-soak them in water for at least 30 minutes.
2. Make the teriyaki sauce by combining teriyaki sauce, sesame oil, lemon juice, brown sugar, ginger, garlic in a small saucepan over medium heat.
3. Mix the cornflour in water until no lumps remain, then stir into the sauce.
4. Cook the sauce until it thickens, stirring frequently, about 2-3 minutes. Remove from heat and set aside to cool.
5. Preheat the air fryer to 180 degrees Celsius.
6. Season salmon cubes with a bit of salt and pepper to taste. Then thread salmon, red peppers, courgettes, and pineapple onto the skewers, alternating until all ingredients are used.
7. Brush each skewer generously with the teriyaki sauce.
8. Place the skewers into the air fryer basket, making sure they are not touching.
9. Cook the skewers in the air fryer for 5-6 minutes, then flip them over and brush with more teriyaki sauce.
10. Continue cooking for another 5-6 minutes or until the salmon is fully cooked and vegetables are tender.
11. Serve immediately while hot, drizzled with the remaining teriyaki sauce.

NUTRITION FACTS PER 100G:
Energy: 104kcal | Protein: 8.2g | Total Fat: 4.5g | Saturated Fat: 0.8g |
Carbohydrates: 6.7g | Sugars: 4.5g | Dietary Fibre: 0.9g

COQ AU VIN BITES

Servings: 6 | Difficulty: Medium | Temperature: 180 degrees Celsius |
Preparation Time: 20 minutes | Cooking Time: 15 minutes

INGREDIENTS:

- ✪ 600g chicken thighs, boneless and skinless
- ✪ 100g streaky bacon
- ✪ 150g button mushrooms
- ✪ 1 small onion, finely chopped
- ✪ 2 garlic cloves, minced
- ✪ 200ml red wine
- ✪ 2 tablespoons plain flour
- ✪ 1 tablespoon olive oil
- ✪ salt and black pepper, to taste
- ✪ 1 tablespoon fresh thyme leaves
- ✪ 2 tablespoons flat-leaf parsley, chopped
- ✪ toothpicks, for serving

PREPARATION:

1. Cut the chicken thighs into bite-sized pieces and set aside.
2. In a large pan, heat the olive oil and add the streaky bacon. Cook until crispy, then remove and set on a paper towel.
3. In the same pan, add the button mushrooms and sauté for around 5 minutes, until they've released their moisture and are golden brown. Remove and set aside.
4. Add the onion and garlic to the pan and cook for approximately 3 minutes, or until the onion becomes transparent.
5. Return the bacon and mushrooms back to the pan, add the chicken pieces and sprinkle with plain flour. Stir until all ingredients are well coated with the flour.
6. Pour in the red wine, mixing well over medium heat until the mixture thickens and reduces. Season with salt, pepper and thyme leaves. Let the mixture cool slightly.
7. Preheat the air fryer to 180 degrees Celsius.
8. Pick up a small amount of the mixture with a spoon, shape into a bite-sized ball and skewer with a toothpick. Repeat until all the mixture is used.
9. Place the Coq au Vin bites into the air fryer in a single layer, ensuring they are not touching. Depending on the size of your air fryer, you may need to do this in batches.
10. Cook the bites for 15 minutes, or until they are golden brown and the chicken is cooked thoroughly.
11. Sprinkle with chopped parsley before serving.

NUTRITION FACTS PER 100G:
Energy: 206kcal | Protein: 22g | Total Fat: 10g | Saturated Fat: 3g |
Carbohydrates: 3g | Sugars: 1g | Dietary Fibre: 0.5g

PANKO-CRUSTED FISH CAKES

Servings: 4 | Difficulty: Medium | Temperature: 190 degrees Celsius |
Preparation Time: 15 minutes | Cooking Time: 15 minutes

INGREDIENTS:

- 450g white fish fillets
- 70g Panko bread crumbs
- 2 tablespoons olive oil
- zest of 1 lemon
- 1 tablespoon chopped parsley
- 1 medium egg
- 70g potatoes, boiled and mashed
- a pinch of salt
- a pinch of black pepper

PREPARATION:

1. Place the fish fillets in a steamer and steam for about 5 minutes, until they're cooked through and flake easily with a fork.
2. Remove the fish from the steamer, and let it cool. Once cooled, flake the fish into a large bowl.
3. Add the mashed potatoes, egg, lemon zest, chopped parsley, salt, and pepper to the bowl with the flaked fish. Mix well until the ingredients are evenly distributed.
4. Form the fish mixture into 8 evenly sized cakes.
5. Spread out the Panko bread crumbs on a flat plate. Roll each fish cake in the breadcrumbs until they're all coated evenly.
6. Transfer the crumbed fish cakes to a plate, and freeze them for about 10 minutes to firm up.
7. While the fish cakes are freezing, preheat your air fryer to 190 degrees Celsius.
8. Brush each side of the fish cakes lightly with olive oil. Arrange the fish cakes in the air fryer basket, making sure not to overcrowd them.
9. Cook the fish cakes in the air fryer for 10 to 15 minutes, or until golden brown and crispy. The cakes should be turned over halfway through cooking to ensure they cook evenly.
10. Once cooked, remove the fish cakes from the air fryer and leave them to cool slightly before serving.

NUTRITION FACTS PER 100G:
Energy: 136kcal | Protein: 13.8g | Total Fat: 5.8g | Saturated Fat: 1.2g |
Carbohydrates: 9.6g | Sugars: 0.8g | Dietary Fibre: 0.6g

CHICKEN AND LEEK POT PIES

Servings: 4 | Difficulty: Medium | Temperature: 190 degrees Celsius |
Preparation Time: 20 minutes | Cooking Time: 25 minutes

INGREDIENTS:

- 450g chicken breast, cut into bite-sized pieces
- 2 medium leeks, sliced
- 1 onion, finely chopped
- 2 cloves of garlic, minced
- 200g puff pastry
- 75g plain flour
- 50g butter
- 400ml chicken stock
- 100ml double cream
- 2 tablespoons olive oil
- 2 tablespoons fresh thyme leaves
- salt and pepper to taste

PREPARATION:

1. Preheat your air fryer to 190 degrees Celsius.
2. In a pan, heat the olive oil and add the chicken pieces. Cook until they're browned on all sides, then remove and set aside.
3. Add butter to the same pan and melt. Stir in the chopped onions and leeks and cook until softened.
4. Add the minced garlic and cook, stirring constantly, for about 30 seconds until fragrant.
5. Sprinkle flour over the vegetable mixture and stir well. Cook for a further two minutes.
6. Gradually pour in the chicken stock, stirring constantly.
7. Mix in the double cream and thyme leaves. Season with salt and pepper.
8. Let the pot pie filling simmer and reduce till it thickens slightly.
9. Return the browned chicken pieces into the pan, stir, and remove from heat.
10. On a floured surface, roll out the puff pastry to fit the top of your pie dishes.
11. Divide the pot pie filling between your pie dishes.
12. Place the puff pastry on top of each dish, crimping the edges to seal.
13. Place your pot pies in the air fryer basket, making sure not to overcrowd.
14. Cook for about 25 minutes, or until the pastry is golden and puffed.
15. Let the pies cool for a few minutes before serving.

NUTRITION FACTS PER 100G:
Energy: 200kcal | Protein: 12g | Total Fat: 12g | Saturated Fat: 5g |
Carbohydrates: 12g | Sugars: 1g | Dietary Fibre: 1g

SPICED TILAPIA WITH MANGO SALSA

Servings: 4 | Difficulty: Medium | Temperature: 180 degrees Celsius |
Preparation Time: 20 minutes | Cooking Time: 10 to 12 minutes

INGREDIENTS:

- 520g tilapia fillets
- 2 tablespoons olive oil
- juice of 1 lime
- 1/2 teaspoon paprika
- 1/2 teaspoon garam masala
- 1/2 teaspoon garlic powder
- 1/4 teaspoon cayenne pepper
- salt and black pepper
- For the Mango Salsa:
- 200g chopped ripe mango
- 50g diced red onion
- 50g diced red pepper
- 15g chopped fresh coriander
- juice of 1 lime
- 1/2 teaspoon salt
- 1/4 teaspoon black pepper

PREPARATION:

1. In a small bowl, mix olive oil, lime juice, paprika, garam masala, garlic powder, cayenne pepper, salt, and black pepper.
2. Rub this spice mixture all over the tilapia fillets, ensuring to coat evenly. Allow the fillets to marinate for about 10 minutes.
3. During this time, prepare the mango salsa. Combine chopped mango, red onion, red pepper, coriander, lime juice, salt, and pepper in a bowl. Stir well and set aside.
4. Place the marinated tilapia fillets in the air fryer basket. Ensure they are placed in a single layer, not overlapping.
5. Set the air fryer to 180 degrees Celsius and cook for 10 to 12 minutes, or until the fish is flaky and cooked through.
6. Once done, carefully remove the fillets from the air fryer. Serve hot, topped with the prepared mango salsa.

NUTRITION FACTS PER 100G:
Energy: 107kcal | Protein: 12.7g | Total Fat: 4.3g | Saturated Fat: 0.7g |
Carbohydrates: 3.8g | Sugars: 2.7g | Dietary Fibre: 0.8g

Chapter 4:
Red Meat and Game (25 recipes)

BEEF WELLINGTON BITES

Servings: 4 | Difficulty: Medium | Temperature: 190 degrees Celsius |
Preparation Time: 25 minutes | Cooking Time: 15 minutes

INGREDIENTS:

- 500g beef fillet, cut into bite-sized pieces
- 1 tablespoon olive oil
- salt and pepper to taste
- 2 tablespoons dijon mustard
- 100g chestnut mushrooms, finely chopped
- 1 shallot, finely chopped
- 1 clove garlic, minced
- 50ml dry white wine
- 200g ready-rolled puff pastry
- 1 egg, beaten

PREPARATION:

1. Season the beef bites with salt and pepper. Then, lightly fry in a pan with 1 tablespoon of olive oil. They should be browned but not fully cooked.
2. Brush the beef with the Dijon mustard. This will help to stick the mushroom mixture to the beef.
3. In the same pan, sauté the chopped shallots, garlic and mushrooms until they are soft, it should take around 5 minutes.
4. Add the wine to the pan, and cook until it's evaporated.
5. Let the mushroom mixture cool. Once it has cooled, blend it in a food processor until it's a paste.
6. Roll out the puff pastry and cut it into squares, large enough to wrap around each piece of beef.
7. Place a piece of beef in the centre of each square. Spoon some of the mushroom paste on top. Then bring the corners of the pastry together to seal the beef and mushroom paste inside. Brush each bite with the beaten egg.
8. Preheat the air fryer to 190 degrees Celsius.
9. Place the Beef Wellington bites into the air fryer and cook for about 15 minutes, until the pastry is golden brown and puffed up.
10. Let the bites rest for a few minutes before serving. They will be hot inside.

NUTRITION FACTS PER 100G:
Energy: 287kcal | Protein: 20.6g | Total Fat: 18.7g | Saturated Fat: 5.3g |
Carbohydrates: 9.1g | Sugars: 0.9g | Dietary Fibre: 0.6g

LAMB KOFTAS

Servings: 4 | Difficulty: Medium | Temperature: 200 degrees Celsius | Preparation Time: 20 minutes | Cooking Time: 15 minutes

INGREDIENTS:

- ✪ 500g minced lamb
- ✪ 1 medium red onion, finely chopped
- ✪ 3 tablespoons parsley, finely chopped
- ✪ 3 tablespoons coriander, finely chopped

- ✪ 2 garlic cloves, minced
- ✪ 1 teaspoon cumin
- ✪ 1 teaspoon ground coriander
- ✪ 1 teaspoon smoked paprika
- ✪ 1/2 teaspoon cinnamon

- ✪ 1/2 teaspoon black pepper
- ✪ salt to taste
- ✪ 4 skewers (if wooden, soaked in water for 30 minutes prior to use)

PREPARATION:

1. In a large mixing bowl, combine the minced lamb, chopped onion, parsley, coriander, minced garlic, cumin, ground coriander, smoked paprika, cinnamon, black pepper, and salt. Mix thoroughly until all ingredients are evenly combined.
2. Divide the meat mixture into 4 equal parts. Take each part and wrap it around a skewer, pressing it gently down the length of the skewer to form a sausage like shape.
3. Place the skewers with the koftas into the freezer for 10 minutes. This will help them maintain their shape while cooking.
4. Preheat your air fryer to 200 degrees Celsius.
5. Place the skewers into the air fryer basket, ensuring they are not touching to allow for even cooking.
6. Cook the koftas at 200 degrees Celsius for 15 minutes, or until they are cooked to your liking. You might want to turn them halfway through the cooking time to ensure all sides are evenly cooked.
7. Once done, carefully remove the koftas from the air fryer and allow them to rest for a few minutes before serving them on a plate.

NUTRITION FACTS PER 100G:
Energy: 260kcal | Protein: 15g | Total Fat: 20g | Saturated Fat: 9g | Carbohydrates: 2g | Sugars: 1g | Dietary Fibre: 1g

PORK AND APPLE BURGERS

Servings: 4 | Difficulty: Easy | Temperature: 180 degrees Celsius | Preparation Time: 15 minutes | Cooking Time: 20 minutes

INGREDIENTS:

- 500g pork mince
- 2 tablespoons olive oil
- 60g breadcrumbs
- 1 medium onion, finely chopped
- 1 medium apple, cored and grated
- 1 large egg, beaten
- 1 teaspoon salt
- 1/2 teaspoon ground black pepper
- 4 burger buns
- 1 large lettuce leaf, shredded
- 4 tablespoons tomato ketchup

PREPARATION:

1. Start by mixing the pork mince, breadcrumbs, onion, apple, egg, salt, and pepper together in a large bowl. Combine all the ingredients thoroughly until the mixture holds together well.
2. Shape the mixture into four equal sized burger patties. Use your hands to flatten the patties to approximately 1.5cm height. Make sure the patties are evenly round and of the same thickness for even cooking.
3. Preheat the air fryer to 180 degrees Celsius for about 3 minutes. Brush the patties lightly with olive oil on both sides to prevent them from sticking to the fryer.
4. Cook the patties in the air fryer for 20 minutes. Ensure to flip them halfway through the cooking time to ensure all sides are evenly cooked.
5. While the patties are cooking, slice open the burger buns without fully separating the two halves. Set aside.
6. Once cooked, carefully remove the patties from the air fryer using a pair of tongs.
7. To serve, place a handful of shredded lettuce on the bottom half of each bun, followed by the patties. Top each patty with a generous tablespoon of tomato ketchup before covering with the top half of the bun.
8. Serve the Pork and Apple Burgers hot for the best dining experience.

NUTRITION FACTS PER 100G:
Energy: 235kcal | Protein: 11g | Total Fat: 16g | Saturated Fat: 5g | Carbohydrates: 10g | Sugars: 3.8g | Dietary Fibre: 0.9g

GAME PIE POCKETS

Servings: 4 | Difficulty: Medium | Temperature: 190 degrees Celsius | Preparation Time: 20 minutes | Cooking Time: 15 minutes

INGREDIENTS:

- 400g minced game meat (venison or rabbit)
- 1 medium onion, finely chopped
- 2 cloves garlic, minced
- 70g garden peas, defrosted
- 2 medium carrots, finely chopped
- 2 tablespoons Worcestershire sauce
- 1 tablespoon olive oil
- salt and pepper to taste
- 500g puff pastry
- 1 beaten egg for egg wash

PREPARATION:

1. Heat the olive oil in a pan over medium heat. Add the onion and garlic and cook until the onion is translucent.
2. Add the minced game to the pan. Cook until the meat is browned, breaking it up as it cooks.
3. Stir in the carrots and peas. Season to taste with salt and pepper. Add the Worcestershire sauce, mix well and cook for a few more minutes until the vegetables are softened.
4. Roll out the puff pastry and cut it into eight squares.
5. Scoop a portion of the meat mixture onto half of each pastry square. Fold the pastry over to form a pocket, sealing the edges with a fork.
6. Preheat the air fryer at 190 degrees Celsius.
7. Brush each pocket with the beaten egg. Place the pockets in the air fryer basket, ensuring they are not touching.
8. Air fry the pockets for about 15 minutes, or until they are golden brown and crisp.
9. Remove the pockets from the air fryer and let them cool for a few minutes before serving.

NUTRITION FACTS PER 100G:
Energy: 270kcal | Protein: 9.8g | Total Fat: 17.6g | Saturated Fat: 6.8g | Carbohydrates: 21.3g | Sugars: 1.2g | Dietary Fibre: 1.7g

LAMB AND MINT SAUSAGES

Servings: 4 | Difficulty: Easy | Temperature: 180 degrees Celsius |
Preparation Time: 15 minutes | Cooking Time: 12 minutes

INGREDIENTS:

- 500g lamb mince
- 1/2 red onion, finely chopped
- 2 garlic cloves, minced
- 2 tablespoons fresh mint, finely chopped
- 1 teaspoon salt
- 1/2 teaspoon black pepper
- 1/2 teaspoon paprika
- 1 tablespoon olive oil

PREPARATION:

1. In a large bowl, place the lamb mince, chopped onion, minced garlic and finely chopped fresh mint.
2. Season the lamb mixture with salt, pepper and paprika. Then, mix thoroughly until all the ingredients are well combined together.
3. Divide the lamb mixture into 8 evenly sized sections and shape each one into a sausage. Slightly flatten each sausage for easier cooking.
4. Brush each sausage lightly with olive oil. On the other hand, preheat the air fryer to 180 degrees Celsius.
5. Arrange the sausages in the basket of the air fryer, ensuring not to overcrowd the basket. You may need to cook in batches if your air fryer is not large enough.
6. Cook the sausages for 12 minutes, flipping over halfway through, until well-browned and cooked through.
7. Serve your lamb and mint sausages hot with your preferred dipping sauce or side dish.

NUTRITION FACTS PER 100G:
Energy: 252kcal | Protein: 21g | Total Fat: 18g | Saturated Fat: 7g |
Carbohydrates: 3g | Sugars: 1g | Dietary Fibre: 0.5g

STEAK AND ALE PIE CUPS

Servings: 4 | Difficulty: Medium | Temperature: 200 degrees Celsius |
Preparation Time: 45 minutes | Cooking Time: 15 minutes

INGREDIENTS:

- 400g diced steak
- 500ml ale
- 150g button mushrooms
- 1 large onion, finely chopped
- 2 cloves garlic, minced
- 1 tablespoon Worcestershire sauce
- 1 tablespoon cornflour
- salt and pepper to taste
- 500g puff pastry
- 1 egg, beaten
- 4 tablespoons double cream

PREPARATION:

1. In a saucepan, combine steak, ale, mushrooms, onion, garlic, Worcestershire sauce, salt, and pepper on medium heat until it bubbles.
2. In a small bowl, blend cornflour and some cold water until smooth and stir into the saucepan.
3. Lower the heat, cover, and simmer for about 30 minutes until the steak is tender. Let it cool.
4. Preheat the air fryer to 200 degrees Celsius.
5. Roll out the puff pastry and cut into 4 squares.
6. Press each square into an air fryer basket to form a 'cup'.
7. Fill each pastry cup with the steak mixture.
8. Fold the corners of the pastry over the filling and brush with beaten egg.
9. Air fry for about 15 minutes until the pastry is golden.
10. Warm the double cream in a saucepan over low heat and pour over each pie before serving.

NUTRITION FACTS PER 100G:
Energy: 230kcal | Protein: 8.5g | Total Fat: 14.7g | Saturated Fat: 5.6g |
Carbohydrates: 15.7g | Sugars: 1.3g | Dietary Fibre: 0.8g

CHILLI CON CARNE BOWLS

Servings: 4 | Difficulty: Medium | Temperature: 175 degrees Celsius |
Preparation Time: 10 minutes | Cooking Time: 20 minutes

INGREDIENTS:

- 500g minced beef
- 1 medium onion, chopped
- 2 cloves of garlic, minced
- 1 red pepper, diced
- 2 teaspoons chilli powder
- 1 teaspoon cumin
- 400g tin of chopped tomatoes
- 400g tin of kidney beans, drained
- 200ml beef stock
- 2 tablespoons olive oil
- salt and pepper to taste
- fresh coriander for garnish

PREPARATION:

1. Preheat the air fryer to 175 degrees Celsius.
2. Heat the olive oil in a pan over medium heat, then add the onion and garlic, frying until translucent.
3. Add the minced beef to the pan and cook until browned.
4. Add the red pepper, chilli powder, and cumin, stirring until well mixed.
5. Transfer the mix to the air fryer basket. Add the chopped tomatoes, kidney beans, and beef stock, stirring well. Season with salt and pepper.
6. Cook in the air fryer for 20 minutes until bubbling and thickened.
7. Serve hot, garnish with fresh coriander.

NUTRITION FACTS PER 100G:
Energy: 105kcal | Protein: 7g | Total Fat: 6g | Saturated Fat: 2.2g |
Carbohydrates: 4.6g | Sugars: 2g | Dietary Fibre: 1.3g

AIR-FRIED LIVER AND ONIONS

Servings: 4 | Difficulty: Medium | Temperature: 180 degrees Celsius |
Preparation Time: 10 minutes | Cooking Time: 15 minutes

INGREDIENTS:

- ✪ 450g calves' liver
- ✪ 2 large onions
- ✪ 2 tablespoons olive oil
- ✪ 1 teaspoon sea salt
- ✪ 1 teaspoon pepper
- ✪ 1 teaspoon thyme

PREPARATION:

1. Preheat your air fryer to 180 degrees Celsius.
2. Thinly slice the onions.
3. Toss them in a bowl with olive oil, sea salt and thyme.
4. Place the onions in the air fryer basket and cook for 7-8 minutes or until golden brown.
5. In the meantime, rinse the liver and pat it dry.
6. Season with sea salt and pepper.
7. Once the onions are cooked, remove them from the air fryer and set aside.
8. Place the liver in the air fryer basket and cook for about 4-5 minutes per side.
9. Add the onions back to the air fryer in the last 2 minutes of the liver's cooking time.
10. Serve immediately, ensuring the liver is fully cooked before eating.

NUTRITION FACTS PER 100G:
Energy: 157kcal | Protein: 17.5g | Total Fat: 8.1g | Saturated Fat: 2.3g |
Carbohydrates: 5.2g | Sugars: 1.8g | Dietary Fibre: 1.0g

BEEF STROGANOFF SKEWERS

Servings: 4 | Difficulty: Easy | Temperature: 190 degrees Celsius |
Preparation Time: 20 minutes | Cooking Time: 12 minutes

INGREDIENTS:

- 500g beef (cut into 2.5cm pieces)
- 10 wooden skewers
- 300g mushrooms (sliced)
- 1 tablespoon olive oil
- 2 tablespoons soy sauce
- 1 tablespoon dijon mustard
- 200ml double cream
- 2 garlic cloves (minced)
- salt and pepper to taste

PREPARATION:

1. Soak wooden skewers in water for 10 minutes.
2. While skewers are soaking, combine beef, mushrooms, olive oil, soy sauce, dijon mustard, minced garlic, salt and pepper. Ensure all pieces are evenly coated.
3. Thread pieces of beef and mushrooms alternately onto skewers.
4. Preheat the air fryer to 190 degrees Celsius.
5. Arrange skewers in the air fryer basket, ensuring they aren't touching.
6. Cook at 190 degrees Celsius for 10 minutes.
7. After 10 minutes, remove skewers from air fryer and set them on a plate.
8. Pour double cream into skillet and heat on medium heat until warm.
9. Dip each skewer into the warm cream before serving.

NUTRITION FACTS PER 100G:
Energy: 155kcal | Protein: 10g | Total Fat: 9g | Saturated Fat: 3.5g |
Carbohydrates: 1.8g | Sugars: 1g | Dietary Fibre: 0.4g

TRADITIONAL CORNED BEEF HASH

Servings: 4 | Difficulty: Medium | Temperature: 180 degrees Celsius |
Preparation Time: 15 minutes | Cooking Time: 15 minutes

INGREDIENTS:

- ✪ 450g corned beef, diced
- ✪ 500g potatoes, peeled and diced
- ✪ 1 large onion, diced
- ✪ 2 tablespoons olive oil
- ✪ 1/2 teaspoon fresh ground black pepper
- ✪ 1/2 teaspoon salt
- ✪ 1 tablespoon fresh parsley, finely chopped
- ✪ 4 eggs (optional)

PREPARATION:

1. Mix the diced potatoes, onions, and corned beef in a large bowl.
2. Drizzle with olive oil, then season with salt and black pepper. Toss well to ensure all ingredients are coated.
3. Transfer the mixture into the air fryer's basket.
4. Cook at 180 degrees Celsius for 10 minutes. Shake the basket then cook for another 5 minutes.
5. Optional: In the last 3 minutes, create space and crack the eggs into the corned beef hash.
6. Sprinkle chopped parsley over the hash before serving.

NUTRITION FACTS PER 100G:
Energy: 210kcal | Protein: 9g | Total Fat: 13g | Saturated Fat: 4g |
Carbohydrates: 15g | Sugars: 1g | Dietary Fibre: 1g

SPICED VENISON STEAKS

Servings: 4 | Difficulty: Medium | Temperature: 200 degrees Celsius |
Preparation Time: 15 minutes | Cooking Time: 15 minutes

INGREDIENTS:

- 4 venison steaks (approx 150g each)
- 2 tablespoons olive oil
- 1 tablespoon cayenne pepper
- 1 tablespoon ground coriander
- 2 teaspoons crushed black pepper
- Salt to taste

PREPARATION:

1. Marinate the venison steaks with olive oil, cayenne pepper, ground coriander, crushed black pepper, and salt. Let it sit for 10 minutes.
2. Preheat the air fryer at 200 degrees Celsius.
3. Lay the marinated venison steaks in the air fryer basket without overlapping.
4. Air fry the venison steaks for 12-15 minutes until they are evenly cooked.
5. Rest the cooked venison steaks for 2-3 minutes before serving.

NUTRITION FACTS PER 100G:
Energy: 193kcal | Protein: 22.5g | Total Fat: 11.5g | Saturated Fat: 3.1g |
Carbohydrates: 2.9g | Sugars: 0.3g | Dietary Fibre: 1.6g

COTTAGE PIE PARCELS

Servings: 4 | Difficulty: Medium | Temperature: 180 degrees Celsius |
Preparation Time: 30 minutes | Cooking Time: 20 minutes

INGREDIENTS:

- 500g minced beef
- 2 tablespoons olive oil
- 1 large onion, finely chopped
- 2 carrots, finely chopped
- 2 sticks celery, finely chopped
- 1 teaspoon dried rosemary
- 300ml beef stock
- 4 ready-made puff pastry squares
- 600g potatoes, peeled and cubed
- 100ml double cream
- 2 tablespoons butter
- salt and pepper to taste
- 1 beaten egg for glaze

PREPARATION:

1. Heat 1 tablespoon olive oil in a pan and brown the minced beef. Set aside.
2. In the same pan, add 1 tablespoon olive oil and sauté onion, carrots, celery, and rosemary until softened.
3. Return the beef to the pan, add the beef stock, and let it simmer until the liquid has reduced. Season with salt and pepper.
4. While the beef is simmering, boil the potatoes until soft. Drain and mash with double cream and butter. Season with salt and pepper.
5. Preheat the air fryer to 180 degrees Celsius.
6. Place a spoonful of the beef mixture in the centre of each pastry square, top with a spoonful of mashed potatoes.
7. Fold the pastry over to form a parcel. Seal the edges with a fork.
8. Brush each parcel with the beaten egg.
9. Air-Fry the parcels for 20 minutes, or until golden and crisp.
10. Serve the Cottage Pie Parcels hot.

NUTRITION FACTS PER 100G:
Energy: 150kcal | Protein: 8g | Total Fat: 7g | Saturated Fat: 3g |
Carbohydrates: 10g | Sugars: 1g | Dietary Fibre: 1.5g

MUSTARD-GLAZED PORK CHOPS

Servings: 4 | Difficulty: Medium | Temperature: 200 Degrees Celsius |
Preparation Time: 10 minutes | Cooking Time: 20 minutes

INGREDIENTS:

- 4 boneless pork chops (approximately 800g)
- salt to taste
- pepper to taste
- 60ml whole grain mustard
- 2 tablespoons honey
- 1 tablespoon Worcestershire sauce
- 1 tablespoon apple cider vinegar
- 1 tablespoon olive oil
- fresh rosemary for garnish

PREPARATION:

1. Pat dry the pork chops and season well with salt and pepper on both sides.
2. Preheat Air Fryer at 200 Degrees Celsius for 3-5 minutes.
3. Combine mustard, honey, Worcestershire sauce, and apple cider vinegar in a small bowl. Set aside.
4. Lightly brush both sides of the pork chops with olive oil.
5. Place pork chops in the Air Fryer, ensuring they don't overlap.
6. Cook at 200 Degrees Celsius for 10 minutes.
7. Flip the pork chops, brush them generously with the mustard glaze and cook for an additional 10 minutes or until chops reach an internal temperature of 63 Degrees Celsius.
8. Allow pork chops to rest for a few minutes before serving.
9. Garnish with fresh rosemary and serve hot.

NUTRITION FACTS PER 100G:
Energy: 211kcal | Protein: 28g | Total Fat: 8g | Saturated Fat: 2.3g |
Carbohydrates: 4g | Sugars: 3g | Dietary Fibre: 0.5g

BEEF AND HORSERADISH YORKSHIRE PUDDINGS

Servings: 4 | Difficulty: Medium | Temperature: 180 degrees Celsius |
Preparation Time: 25 minutes | Cooking Time: 15 minutes

INGREDIENTS:

- 100g plain flour
- 2 eggs
- 150ml milk
- 1 tablespoon vegetable oil
- 200g roast beef slices
- 4 tablespoons horseradish sauce

PREPARATION:

1. In a bowl, whisk together the plain flour, eggs, and milk until smooth.
2. Preheat the air fryer to 180 degrees Celsius.
3. Grease four holes of an air fryer-safe pudding mould with vegetable oil.
4. Divide the batter evenly among the mould holes.
5. Cook in the preheated air fryer for about 15 minutes until the puddings have risen and are golden brown.
6. Heat the roast beef slices in the air fryer for 3-5 minutes at the same temperature.
7. When the Yorkshire puddings are ready, remove them from the moulds and cut a slit in the top of each to create a pocket.
8. Fill each pudding with the warmed roast beef slices, top with a dollop of horseradish sauce. Serve immediately.

NUTRITION FACTS PER 100G:
Energy: 190kcal | Protein: 11g | Total Fat: 9g | Saturated Fat: 3g |
Carbohydrates: 13g | Sugars: 1.5g | Dietary Fibre: 0.5g

SHEPHERD'S PIE BITES

Servings: 4 | Difficulty: Medium | Temperature: 180 degrees Celsius |
Preparation Time: 25 minutes | Cooking Time: 15 minutes

INGREDIENTS:

- 500g minced lamb
- 1 small onion, chopped
- 2 cloves of garlic, minced
- 1 carrot, chopped
- 80g frozen peas
- 240ml beef stock
- 2 tablespoons tomato purée
- 1 teaspoon Worcestershire sauce
- 2 teaspoons dried mixed herbs
- salt and pepper to taste
- 500g potatoes, peeled and diced
- 50g unsalted butter
- 60ml milk
- 80g shredded cheddar cheese
- cooking spray

PREPARATION:

1. In a large pan, cook lamb, onion, garlic, and carrots over medium heat until lamb is browned and vegetables are tender.
2. Add peas, beef stock, tomato purée, Worcestershire sauce, mixed herbs, salt, and pepper, cook for 15 minutes, then set aside.
3. Boil potatoes in a large pot of salted water until tender, then drain and mash with butter and milk.
4. Preheat the air fryer to 180 degrees Celsius.
5. Using a mini muffin tray sprayed with cooking spray, press mashed potatoes into each cup, forming a crust.
6. Spoon the lamb mixture into each potato crust and top with shredded cheddar.
7. Place the tray in the preheated air fryer and cook for 15 minutes until cheese is bubbling and golden.
8. Allow to cool for a few minutes before removing from the tray and serve.

NUTRITION FACTS PER 100G:
Energy: 135kcal | Protein: 8g | Total Fat: 7g | Saturated Fat: 3g |
Carbohydrates: 9g | Sugars: 1g | Dietary Fibre: 1g

MINTED LAMB CHOPS

Servings: 4 | Difficulty: Easy | Temperature: 200 degrees Celsius |
Preparation Time: 40 minutes | Cooking Time: 12 minutes

INGREDIENTS:

- 400g lamb chops
- 2 tablespoons olive oil
- 3 tablespoons lemon juice
- 2 tablespoons fresh mint leaves, finely chopped
- 2 garlic cloves, minced
- salt and pepper to taste

PREPARATION:

1. Rinse the lamb chops and pat dry with kitchen paper.
2. In a bowl, mix together the olive oil, lemon juice, chopped mint leaves, minced garlic, salt and pepper.
3. Add the lamb chops to the bowl and thoroughly coat with the mint marinade.
4. Cover the bowl and let the chops marinate in the fridge for a minimum of 30 minutes.
5. Preheat the air fryer to 200 degrees Celsius.
6. Place the lamb chops in the air fryer basket ensuring they don't overlap.
7. Cook for 6 minutes, then flip the chops over and cook for a further 6 minutes.
8. Check the lamb is cooked to your liking; if necessary, cook for a further 2-3 minutes for well done.
9. Allow the chops to rest for a few minutes before serving.

NUTRITION FACTS PER 100G:
Energy: 235kcal | Protein: 23.4g | Total Fat: 14.2g | Saturated Fat: 5.2g |
Carbohydrates: 3.0g | Sugars: 1.3g | Dietary Fibre: 0.3g

BEEF AND GUINNESS STEW CUPS

Servings: 6 | Difficulty: Medium | Temperature: 180 degrees Celsius |
Preparation Time: 20 minutes | Cooking Time: 30 minutes

INGREDIENTS:

- 400g stewing beef, cut into bite-sized pieces
- 300ml Guinness
- 2 tablespoons olive oil
- 1 medium onion, chopped
- 2 cloves garlic, minced
- 200g carrots, chopped
- 200g potatoes, chopped
- 1 tablespoon tomato paste
- 1 tablespoon Worcestershire sauce
- 1 teaspoon thyme
- salt and pepper to taste
- pre-made puff pastry
- 1 egg, beaten

PREPARATION:

1. Preheat your air fryer to 180 degrees Celsius.
2. Heat the olive oil in a pan and brown the beef on all sides.
3. Add the onion, garlic, carrots, and potatoes to the pan, cooking until soft.
4. Stir in the tomato paste, Worcestershire sauce, thyme, salt, and pepper.
5. Pour in the Guinness, bring the mixture to a simmer and cook for about 10 minutes until the sauce thickens.
6. Roll out the puff pastry and cut into circles large enough to line the cups of a muffin tin.
7. Spoon the beef mixture into the pastry-lined muffin cups.
8. Top each cup with a smaller circle of puff pastry, crimp the edges to seal, and brush with the beaten egg.
9. Air fry the stew cups for about 20-30 minutes until the pastry is golden brown.
10. Remove from the air fryer and allow the stew cups to cool for a few minutes before serving.

NUTRITION FACTS PER 100G:
Energy: 132kcal | Protein: 9.3g | Total Fat: 5.6g | Saturated Fat: 2.1g |
Carbohydrates: 7.8g | Sugars: 1.4g | Dietary Fibre: 1.1g

CRISPY PORK BELLY SLICES

Servings: 4 | Difficulty: Easy | Temperature: 200 degrees Celsius |
Preparation Time: 15 minutes | Cooking Time: 30 minutes

INGREDIENTS:

- 500g pork belly slices
- 2 tablespoons soy sauce
- 1 tablespoon maple syrup
- 2 tablespoons wine vinegar
- 1 teaspoon ground coriander
- 1 teaspoon ground pepper
- 1 teaspoon salt

PREPARATION:

1. Score the pork belly slices on the skin side, be careful not to cut into the meat.
2. In a bowl, combine soy sauce, maple syrup, wine vinegar, ground coriander, pepper, and salt. Mix well.
3. Marinade the pork belly slices in the sauce mixture for at least 10 minutes.
4. Preheat the air fryer to 200 degrees Celsius.
5. Place the marinated pork belly slices in the air fryer, skin side up.
6. Cook for 30 minutes, or until the skin is crisp and golden brown.
7. Take out the pork belly slices from the air fryer and let them rest for a few minutes before serving.

NUTRITION FACTS PER 100G:
Energy: 279kcal | Protein: 15.9g | Total Fat: 21.1g | Saturated Fat: 7.5g |
Carbohydrates: 3.4g | Sugars: 2.2g | Dietary Fibre: 0.1g

AIR-FRIED BANGERS AND MASH

Servings: 4 | Difficulty: Easy | Temperature: 200 degrees Celsius |
Preparation Time: 15 minutes | Cooking Time: 20 minutes

INGREDIENTS:

- 8 large sausages
- 800g potatoes, peeled and chopped
- 50g unsalted butter
- 100ml double cream
- salt and pepper to taste
- 1 tablespoon olive oil
- 200g frozen peas
- 2 tablespoons cornflour
- 350ml beef stock

PREPARATION:

1. Preheat the air fryer to 200 degrees Celsius.
2. Add the sausages and olive oil to the air fryer basket, then cook for 10 minutes, turning halfway through.
3. Meanwhile, boil the potatoes in salted water until tender, then drain and mash together with the butter, double cream, and salt and pepper to taste.
4. Cook the frozen peas in boiling water according to pack instructions, then drain.
5. Mix the cornflour with a little cold water to make a paste, then stir into the beef stock and bring to the boil, stirring until thickened.
6. Serve the sausages over the mashed potatoes, top with the gravy, and serve the peas on the side.

NUTRITION FACTS PER 100G:
Energy: 140kcal | Protein: 5g | Total Fat: 9g | Saturated Fat: 4g |
Carbohydrates: 8g | Sugars: 1g | Dietary Fibre: 1g

SPAGHETTI BOLOGNESE CUPS

Servings: 4 | Difficulty: Medium | Temperature: 200 degrees Celsius |
Preparation Time: 20 minutes | Cooking Time: 30 minutes

INGREDIENTS:

- 500g spaghetti
- 1 tablespoon olive oil
- 400g minced beef
- 1 onion, finely chopped
- 2 cloves of garlic, minced
- 400g can chopped tomatoes
- 100ml red wine
- 2 tablespoons Worcestershire sauce
- 100g grated parmesan cheese
- salt and pepper to taste

PREPARATION:

1. Boil the spaghetti until al dente, drain, and set aside.
2. Preheat your air fryer to 200 degrees Celsius.
3. While the spaghetti is cooling, heat the olive oil in a pan over medium heat.
4. Add the minced beef to the pan and cook until browned.
5. Drain excess fat from the pan and add the onion, cooking until softened.
6. Stir in the garlic, chopped tomatoes, red wine, and Worcestershire sauce.
7. Continue to simmer until the sauce has thickened slightly and season with salt and pepper.
8. Combine cooked spaghetti with the sauce and place equal portions into four separate silicone moulds.
9. Top each mould with grated Parmesan cheese.
10. Place moulds in the air fryer and cook for about 15 minutes or until cheese is golden and bubbling.
11. Carefully remove from the air fryer and allow to cool slightly before serving.

NUTRITION FACTS PER 100G:
Energy: 153kcal | Protein: 8.1g | Total Fat: 6.1g | Saturated Fat: 2.3g |
Carbohydrates: 15.7g | Sugars: 1.9g | Dietary Fibre: 1.3g

HONEY AND MUSTARD GLAZED HAM

Servings: 4-6 | Difficulty: Medium | Temperature: 180 degrees Celsius |
Preparation Time: 15 minutes | Cooking Time: 20 minutes

INGREDIENTS:

- 1kg ham joint
- 60ml clear honey
- 2 tablespoons wholegrain mustard
- 2 tablespoons dark brown soft sugar
- 1/2 teaspoon ground cloves
- salt, to taste
- pepper, to taste

PREPARATION:

1. Pat the ham joint dry, then season with salt and pepper. Preheat the air fryer to 180 degrees Celsius.
2. Mix together the honey, mustard, brown sugar and ground cloves in a bowl. This will form a glaze.
3. Apply half of the glaze evenly over the ham joint.
4. Cook the ham joint in the air fryer for 10 minutes.
5. After 10 minutes, remove the ham from the air fryer. Apply the remaining glaze all over.
6. Return the ham to the air fryer and cook for another 10 minutes until it becomes crispy and golden.
7. Let the ham rest for a few minutes before carving and serving.

NUTRITION FACTS PER 100G:
Energy: 278kcal | Protein: 21g | Total Fat: 17g | Saturated Fat: 5.1g |
Carbohydrates: 7.9g | Sugars: 7.8g | Dietary Fibre: 0.2g

ROAST BEEF AND YORKSHIRE PUDDING WRAPS

Servings: 4 | Difficulty: Medium | Temperature: 180 degrees Celsius |
Preparation Time: 25 minutes | Cooking Time: 40 minutes

INGREDIENTS:

- 800g beef sirloin roast
- 2 tablespoons olive oil
- salt and pepper to taste
- 4 Yorkshire puddings, ready-made
- 100g mixed lettuce leaves
- 1 red onion, thinly sliced
- 2 teaspoons wholegrain mustard
- 4 tablespoons horseradish sauce
- 1 teaspoon thyme
- 1 teaspoon rosemary

PREPARATION:

1. Pat dry the roast beef with kitchen paper, then rub with olive oil, thyme, rosemary, salt, and pepper.
2. Pre-heat the air fryer at 180 degrees Celsius.
3. Place the roast beef in the air fryer and cook for 30 minutes for medium-rare or longer if preferred.
4. Once cooked, remove the roast beef from the air fryer and let it rest for 10 minutes.
5. While the beef is resting, cook the Yorkshire puddings as per packet instructions in the air fryer.
6. Thinly slice the roast beef.
7. Lay out a Yorkshire pudding, spread 1/2 teaspoon of wholegrain mustard and 1 tablespoon of horseradish sauce on each one.
8. Add a handful of mixed lettuce leaves and a few slices of red onion.
9. Top with the sliced roast beef.
10. Fold up the Yorkshire pudding to form a wrap and serve.

NUTRITION FACTS PER 100G:
Energy: 150kcal | Protein: 17.5g | Total Fat: 5.5g | Saturated Fat: 2.1g |
Carbohydrates: 4.7g | Sugars: 1.8g | Dietary Fibre: 0.6g

CLASSIC TOAD IN THE HOLE

Servings: 4 | Difficulty: Medium | Temperature: 180 degrees Celsius |
Preparation Time: 15 minutes | Cooking Time: 25 minutes

INGREDIENTS:

- ✪ 8 traditional pork sausages
- ✪ 100g plain flour
- ✪ 2 large eggs
- ✪ 300ml whole milk
- ✪ 1 tablespoon vegetable oil
- ✪ salt and pepper to taste

PREPARATION:

1. Start off by cooking the sausages in the air fryer set at 180 degrees Celsius for about 10 minutes, until they're browned.
2. Meanwhile, in a large bowl, combine the flour, eggs, milk, and a pinch each of salt and pepper. Whisk until smooth.
3. Once the sausages are done, carefully remove the cooking basket.
4. Pour the oil into an air-fryer-safe dish that fits into the basket.
5. Arrange the cooked sausages evenly in the dish.
6. Pour the batter over the sausages in the dish, leaving a little space at the top to allow for rising.
7. Carefully place the dish back into the air fryer.
8. Cook at 180 degrees Celsius for approximately 25 minutes, or until the batter is risen and golden.
9. Your toad in the hole is ready. Serve it straight from the dish, ensuring to dish out a sausage and some batter for everyone.

NUTRITION FACTS PER 100G:
Energy: 280kcal | Protein: 9.6g | Total Fat: 18.8g | Saturated Fat: 6.1g |
Carbohydrates: 18.2g | Sugars: 2.4g | Dietary Fibre: 0.8g

CARAMELISED ONION AND SAUSAGE ROLLS

Servings: 4 | Difficulty: Medium | Temperature: 180 degrees Celsius |
Preparation Time: 45 minutes | Cooking Time: 15-20 minutes

INGREDIENTS:

- ✪ 500g pork sausages
- ✪ 2 large onions, thinly sliced
- ✪ 2 tablespoons olive oil
- ✪ 1 tablespoon granulated sugar
- ✪ 1 teaspoon salt
- ✪ 20g dijon mustard
- ✪ 375g puff pastry sheet
- ✪ 1 egg, beaten
- ✪ 1 tablespoon poppy seeds

PREPARATION:

1. Heat the olive oil in a frying pan over medium heat. Add onions, sugar, and salt. Cook for about 15 minutes until onions are caramelised.
2. In the meantime, remove the skins from the sausages.
3. In a bowl, combine caramelised onions and sausages. Add Dijon mustard and mix well.
4. Roll out the puff pastry on a flour-dusted surface. Shape the sausage mixture into a log along one edge of the pastry, then roll up tightly.
5. Cut the sausage roll into four equal parts.
6. Brush each sausage roll with the beaten egg and sprinkle with poppy seeds.
7. Preheat the air fryer to 180 degrees Celsius and cook the sausage rolls for 15-20 minutes, or until golden brown and crisp.

NUTRITION FACTS PER 100G:
Energy: 310kcal | Protein: 8g | Total Fat: 24g | Saturated Fat: 6g |
Carbohydrates: 20g | Sugars: 2g | Dietary Fibre: 1g

LAMB TAGINE POCKETS

Servings: 4 | Difficulty: Medium | Temperature: 180 degrees Celsius |
Preparation Time: 20 minutes | Cooking Time: 15 minutes

INGREDIENTS:

- 500g lamb mince
- 2 teaspoons cumin
- 2 teaspoons coriander
- salt to taste
- 4 large pitta breads
- 2 tablespoons olive oil
- 125ml double cream
- 100g couscous
- 2 tablespoons tomato puree
- 1 large onion, finely chopped

PREPARATION:

1. Mix the lamb mince with cumin, coriander, salt, and tomato puree.
2. Sauté onions in 1 tablespoon of olive oil till soft, then add to the meat mixture.
3. Prepare couscous as per package instructions, then mix with the lamb mixture.
4. Slice an opening at one end of each pitta bread and stuff with the lamb-couscous blend.
5. Brush the pitta pockets with the remaining olive oil.
6. Preheat the air fryer at 180 degrees Celsius.
7. Place the stuffed pitta pockets in the air fryer, making sure they are not overlapped.
8. Air fry for about 15 minutes or until the pockets are crispy and brown.
9. Serve hot with double cream.

NUTRITION FACTS PER 100G:
Energy: 240kcal | Protein: 13g | Total Fat: 15g | Saturated Fat: 6g |
Carbohydrates: 13g | Sugars: 2g | Dietary Fibre: 1g

Chapter 5:
Vegetarian and Vegan Choices (20 recipes)

AIR-FRIED BUBBLE AND SQUEAK

Servings: 4 | Difficulty: Easy | Temperature: 185 degrees Celsius |
Preparation Time: 30 minutes | Cooking Time: 20 minutes

INGREDIENTS:

- ✪ 600g cold, cooked potatoes
- ✪ 250g cooked white cabbage
- ✪ 50g unsalted butter
- ✪ 1 onion, finely chopped
- ✪ 1 teaspoon table salt
- ✪ 1 teaspoon ground black pepper
- ✪ 1 tablespoon vegetable oil

PREPARATION:

1. Finely chop potatoes and cabbage. Mix together in a large bowl.
2. Melt butter in a pan over medium heat. Add onion and cook until soft and golden.
3. Add cooked onion, salt, and pepper to the potato and cabbage mix. Stir well to combine.
4. Mould the mixture into four equal patties.
5. Preheat your air fryer to 185 degrees Celsius.
6. Brush each side of the patties with vegetable oil.
7. Place the patties in the air fryer and cook for 20 minutes, or until golden and crisp. Serve immediately.

NUTRITION FACTS PER 100G:
Energy: 76kcal | Protein: 1.6g | Total Fat: 2.4g | Saturated Fat: 1.1g |
Carbohydrates: 11g | Sugars: 1.5g | Dietary Fibre: 2.0g

STUFFED BELL PEPPERS

Servings: 4 | Difficulty: Medium | Temperature: 190 degrees Celsius |
Preparation Time: 20 minutes | Cooking Time: 15 minutes

INGREDIENTS:

- 4 bell peppers
- 300g minced beef
- 1 onion, finely chopped
- 2 garlic cloves, minced
- 200g tinned chopped tomatoes
- 100g cooked rice
- 1 teaspoon chilli powder
- 1 teaspoon cumin
- 100g cheddar cheese, grated
- salt and pepper, to taste
- 2 tablespoons olive oil

PREPARATION:

1. Cut the tops off the bell peppers, remove seeds and set aside.
2. In a pan, heat 1 tablespoon of oil and fry the onion and garlic until softened.
3. Add the minced beef to the pan and cook until browned.
4. Stir in the tinned tomatoes, cooked rice, chilli powder, cumin, and season with salt and pepper. Cook for another 5 minutes.
5. Fill each bell pepper with the beef and rice mixture.
6. Sprinkle the top of each pepper with the grated cheese.
7. Place the stuffed peppers in the air fryer basket. Drizzle over the remaining oil.
8. Cook in the air fryer at 190 degrees Celsius for 15 minutes or until the peppers are tender and the cheese is melted and slightly browned.
9. Serve the stuffed bell peppers hot.

NUTRITION FACTS PER 100G:
Energy: 155kcal | Protein: 7.5g | Total Fat: 10g | Saturated Fat: 3.8g |
Carbohydrates: 7.1g | Sugars: 3.1g | Dietary Fibre: 1.9g

VEGETABLE AND LENTIL CURRY BOWLS

Servings: 4 | Difficulty: Medium | Temperature: 200 degrees Celsius |
Preparation Time: 10 minutes | Cooking Time: 20 minutes

INGREDIENTS:

- 200g dry split red lentils
- 1 large aubergine, diced
- 1 large red pepper, diced
- 1 large courgette, diced
- 1 large onion, chopped
- 4 cloves of garlic, minced
- 1 tablespoon curry powder
- 1 tablespoon turmeric
- 500ml vegetable stock
- salt and pepper, to taste
- 2 tablespoons olive oil
- fresh coriander, for garnish

PREPARATION:

1. Rinse the lentils and leave them to drain.
2. Place aubergine, red pepper, courgette, onion, and garlic into the air fryer basket.
3. Sprinkle vegetables with curry powder, turmeric, salt and pepper, then drizzle with olive oil.
4. Toss to ensure vegetables are evenly coated with spices and oil.
5. Set the air fryer to 200 degrees Celsius and cook for 10 minutes.
6. After 10 minutes, shake the basket and add the lentils to the vegetable mix.
7. Pour the vegetable stock over top, ensuring lentils are completely submerged.
8. Cook for another 10 minutes at 200 degrees Celsius or until lentils are tender.
9. Once done, let it cool for a few minutes before serving.
10. Garnish with fresh coriander and serve in bowls.

NUTRITION FACTS PER 100G:
Energy: 97kcal | Protein: 5.3g | Total Fat: 1.7g | Saturated Fat: 0.2g |
Carbohydrates: 13.7g | Sugars: 3.7g | Dietary Fibre: 5.8g

SPICED CHICKPEA PATTIES

Servings: 4 | Difficulty: Medium | Temperature: 200 degrees Celsius | Preparation Time: 20 minutes | Cooking Time: 15 minutes

INGREDIENTS:

- 400g tinned chickpeas, drained and rinsed
- 2 tablespoons olive oil
- 1 small onion, finely chopped
- 2 cloves garlic, minced
- 1 teaspoon ground cumin
- 1 teaspoon ground coriander
- 1/2 teaspoon chilli flakes
- 2 tablespoons plain flour
- salt and pepper to taste
- fresh coriander leaves, finely chopped (optional)

PREPARATION:

1. Place chickpeas in a bowl and mash with potato masher until chunky.
2. Heat 1 tablespoon of olive oil in a frying pan, add onion, and fry until golden.
3. Add garlic, cumin, coriander, and chilli flakes to the pan. Fry for a minute.
4. Transfer the onion and spice mixture to the bowl with chickpeas.
5. Add flour, salt, pepper and fresh coriander leaves (optional) to the bowl. Mix until well combined.
6. Form the mixture into four patties.
7. Brush the air fryer basket with remaining olive oil.
8. Place the patties in the air fryer basket and cook at 200 degrees Celsius for 15 minutes, or until golden and crispy.
9. Serve the spiced chickpea patties hot with your favourite dipping sauce.

NUTRITION FACTS PER 100G:
Energy: 120kcal | Protein: 4.5g | Total Fat: 4g | Saturated Fat: 0.6g | Carbohydrates: 15g | Sugars: 1.5g | Dietary Fibre: 4g

VEGAN SAUSAGE ROLLS

Servings: 8 rolls | Difficulty: Medium | Temperature: 180 degrees Celsius |
Preparation Time: 25 minutes | Cooking Time: 15 minutes

INGREDIENTS:

- ✪ 250g vegan sausages
- ✪ 1 tablespoon olive oil
- ✪ 1 onion, finely chopped
- ✪ 2 cloves garlic, crushed
- ✪ 1 teaspoon dried sage
- ✪ 1 tablespoon chopped fresh parsley
- ✪ salt and pepper to taste
- ✪ 500g ready-made vegan puff pastry
- ✪ 50g dairy-free milk
- ✪ 1 tablespoon sesame seeds

PREPARATION:

1. Cook the vegan sausages in a saucepan until browned; set aside.
2. In the same pan, add the olive oil and sauté the onion and garlic until they become tender.
3. Add the sage and parsley to the pan, season with salt and pepper, and stir well. Remove the pan from the heat.
4. Unroll the puff pastry and cut it into 8 even-sized rectangles.
5. Crumble the cooked sausages and mix with the onion mixture. Divide this sausage mix equally among each pastry rectangle.
6. Roll the pastry rectangles tightly around the sausage mixture, then brush the edges with some dairy-free milk to seal them.
7. Preheat the air fryer to 180 degrees Celsius.
8. Pinch the edges of the rolls to seal them tight and prevent any filling from escaping during the cooking. Cut a few small slits on the top of each roll.
9. Arrange the rolls in the air fryer basket and brush the tops with more dairy-free milk, then sprinkle with sesame seeds.
10. Cook for 15 minutes in the air fryer or until the pastry is golden and crispy. Serve the vegan sausage rolls hot, accompanied by ketchup or brown sauce, as preferred.

NUTRITION FACTS PER 100G:
Energy: 263kcal | Protein: 6.4g | Total Fat: 16.7g | Saturated Fat: 4.1g |
Carbohydrates: 24.3g | Sugars: 1.1g | Dietary Fibre: 1.6g

CHEESE AND ONION PIE BITES

Servings: 12 bites | Difficulty: Medium | Temperature: 200 degrees Celsius | Preparation Time: 25 minutes | Cooking Time: 12 minutes

INGREDIENTS:

- 350g ready-made short crust pastry
- 200g grated mature cheddar cheese
- 1 large onion, finely chopped
- 2 tablespoons double cream
- 1 egg, beaten
- 1 tablespoon freshly chopped parsley
- salt and pepper to taste

PREPARATION:

1. Roll out the pastry and cut 12 circles using a cookie cutter.
2. Press each circle into a muffin tin to create a mini pastry shell.
3. Preheat your air fryer to 200 degrees Celsius.
4. In a bowl, mix together the cheese, onion, parsley, double cream, salt, and pepper.
5. Spoon the cheese and onion mixture evenly into each pastry shell.
6. Brush the edges of the pastry with the beaten egg.
7. Place the muffin tin into the air fryer.
8. Cook for 12 minutes or until the pastry is golden and the filling is hot.
9. Allow to cool slightly before serving.

NUTRITION FACTS PER 100G:
Energy: 312kcal | Protein: 10.5g | Total Fat: 22.8g | Saturated Fat: 11.6g | Carbohydrates: 15.7g | Sugars: 1.6g | Dietary Fibre: 1.1g

PORTOBELLO MUSHROOMS WITH GARLIC AND THYME

Servings: 2 | Difficulty: Easy | Temperature: 200 degrees Celsius | Preparation Time: 10 minutes | Cooking Time: 10 minutes

INGREDIENTS:

- ✪ 2 large Portobello mushrooms (150g)
- ✪ 2 tablespoons olive oil
- ✪ 1 tablespoon fresh thyme leaves
- ✪ 4 garlic cloves, minced
- ✪ salt and pepper, to taste

PREPARATION:

1. Clean the mushrooms with a damp cloth and remove the stems.
2. Arrange the mushrooms in the air fryer basket with the gills up.
3. Mix olive oil, minced garlic, thyme leaves, salt and pepper in a bowl.
4. Drizzle this mixture over the gilled side of the mushrooms.
5. Air fry at 200 degrees Celsius for 10 minutes, or until the mushrooms are tender and juicy.
6. Serve hot and enjoy your garlic and thyme Portobello mushrooms.

NUTRITION FACTS PER 100G:
Energy: 95kcal | Protein: 2g | Total Fat: 7g | Saturated Fat: 1g | Carbohydrates: 5g | Sugars: 2g | Dietary Fibre: 3g

AIR-FRIED VEGAN "FISH" AND CHIPS

Servings: 4 | Difficulty: Medium | Temperature: 200 degrees Celsius |
Preparation Time: 30 minutes | Cooking Time: 20 minutes

INGREDIENTS:

- ✪ 400g firm tofu
- ✪ 1 tablespoon nori flakes
- ✪ 100g panko breadcrumbs
- ✪ 60ml vegetable oil
- ✪ salt, to taste
- ✪ 1 teaspoon smoked paprika
- ✪ 300g Maris piper potatoes, thinly sliced
- ✪ 2 tablespoons cornflour
- ✪ 120ml plant-based milk
- ✪ lemon wedges, to serve

PREPARATION:

1. Pat dry the tofu and slice into chunky pieces. Sprinkle with nori flakes, salt, and set aside.
2. In a shallow dish, combine panko breadcrumbs with smoked paprika.
3. Dip each tofu piece into the plant-based milk, then coat in the breadcrumb mixture.
4. Preheat the air fryer to 200 degrees Celsius.
5. Arrange the tofu pieces in the fryer basket, brush with a little oil, then cook for 10-12 minutes until golden.
6. Meanwhile, in a separate bowl, toss thinly sliced potatoes with cornflour, a little oil, and salt.
7. Once tofu is done, remove from the fryer and set aside.
8. Place potato slices in the fryer basket, and cook for another 10-12 minutes until crisp and golden.
9. Serve the vegan «fish» and chips hot, with lemon wedges on the side.

NUTRITION FACTS PER 100G:
Energy: 213.6kcal | Protein: 9.2g | Total fat: 14.1g | Saturated Fat: 2.1g |
Carbohydrate: 11.3g | Sugars: 1.4g | Dietary Fibre: 2.5g

CAULIFLOWER CHEESE CUPS

Servings: 6 | Difficulty: Easy | Temperature: 180 degrees Celsius |
Preparation Time: 10 minutes | Cooking Time: 15 minutes

INGREDIENTS:

- 300g cauliflower florets
- 100g shredded cheddar cheese
- 1 medium egg
- 1 tablespoon double cream
- 2 tablespoons onion, minced
- salt and pepper to taste

PREPARATION:

1. Boil the cauliflower until it's soft. Cool it down, then mash it until smooth.
2. In a bowl, mix the mashed cauliflower, cheese, egg, double cream, and onion. Season with salt and pepper.
3. Shape the mixture into small cups then place them into the air fryer.
4. Fry at 180 degrees Celsius for 15 minutes or until golden brown and crispy.
5. Serve the cauliflower cheese cups immediately.

NUTRITION FACTS PER 100G:
Energy: 110kcal | Protein: 7g | Total Fat: 8g | Saturated Fat: 4g |
Carbohydrates: 4g | Sugars: 2g | Dietary Fibre: 2g

RATATOUILLE PARCELS

Servings: 4 | Difficulty: Medium | Temperature: 200 degrees Celsius |
Preparation Time: 20 minutes | Cooking Time: 15 minutes

INGREDIENTS:

- 2 medium aubergines
- 1 small courgette
- 2 small red bell peppers
- 1 small yellow bell pepper
- 1 small red onion
- 3 cloves garlic
- 4 tablespoons olive oil
- 1 teaspoon salt
- 1 teaspoon black pepper
- 2 teaspoons dried basil
- 2 teaspoons dried thyme
- 4 sheets of baking parchment

PREPARATION:

1. Rinse the aubergine, courgette, and bell peppers. Chop them into small pieces along with the red onion.
2. Crush the garlic cloves and mix with the vegetables.
3. Drizzle the vegetables with olive oil, sprinkle with salt, pepper, basil, and thyme. Mix well.
4. Divide the vegetable mixture equally between the sheets of baking parchment and fold them into parcels.
5. Preheat the air fryer to 200 degrees Celsius.
6. Place the parcels in the air fryer basket and cook for 15 minutes until the vegetables are tender.
7. Serve the ratatouille parcels hot.

NUTRITION FACTS PER 100G:
Energy: 115kcal | Protein: 1.6g | Total Fat: 7.8g | Saturated Fat: 1.1g |
Carbohydrates: 8.9g | Sugars: 5.3g | Dietary Fibre: 3.6g

SPINACH AND RICOTTA CANNELLONI BITES

Servings: 4 | Difficulty: Medium | Temperature: 180 degrees Celsius |
Preparation Time: 20 minutes | Cooking Time: 12 minutes

INGREDIENTS:

- 250g fresh spinach leaves
- 250g ricotta cheese
- 8 cannelloni tubes
- 1 small onion, finely chopped
- 2 cloves garlic, minced
- 2 tablespoons olive oil
- 50g parmesan cheese, grated
- 1/2 teaspoon ground nutmeg
- salt and freshly ground black pepper to taste
- 350ml marinara sauce
- 50g mozzarella cheese, shredded

PREPARATION:

1. Preheat the air fryer to 180 degrees Celsius.
2. Heat olive oil in a pan and sauté onion and garlic until fragrant.
3. Add spinach to the pan and cook until wilted. Set aside to cool.
4. In a mixing bowl, combine ricotta, nutmeg, grated Parmesan, and seasonings. Add cooled spinach and mix until well combined.
5. Pipe or spoon the spinach and ricotta mixture into the cannelloni tubes.
6. Spoon a layer of marinara sauce onto the bottom of the air fryer basket.
7. Arrange filled cannelloni in a single layer on top of the sauce.
8. Top cannelloni with the remaining marinara sauce and sprinkle with mozzarella.
9. Cook in the air fryer for about 12 minutes, or until the pasta is tender and the cheese is melted and golden.
10. Allow to cool for a few minutes before serving.

NUTRITION FACTS PER 100G:
Energy: 170kcal | Protein: 6g | Total Fat: 12g | Saturated Fat: 5g |
Carbohydrates: 10g | Sugars: 2g | Dietary Fibre: 3g

VEGAN SHEPHERD'S PIE

Servings: 4 | Difficulty: Medium | Temperature: 180 degrees Celsius |
Preparation Time: 20 minutes | Cooking Time: 20 minutes

INGREDIENTS:

- 600g sweet potatoes, peeled and cut into chunks
- 2 tablespoons olive oil
- 1 onion, chopped
- 2 cloves of garlic, minced
- 200g mushrooms, sliced
- 150g frozen peas
- 2 celery stalks, chopped
- 2 tablespoons tomato purée
- 1 teaspoon dried rosemary
- 1 teaspoon dried thyme
- salt to taste
- ground black pepper to taste
- 100ml vegetable stock

PREPARATION:

1. Boil the sweet potatoes for 15 minutes until tender, drain, and mash together with 1 tablespoon olive oil. Set aside.
2. Preheat the air fryer to 180 degrees Celsius.
3. In a frying pan, heat 1 tablespoon olive oil, add the onion, garlic, and cook until softened.
4. Add the mushrooms, peas, celery to the pan and cook for a further 5 minutes.
5. Stir in the tomato purée, rosemary, thyme, salt, pepper, and vegetable stock. Simmer for 10 minutes until thickened.
6. Transfer the vegetable mixture into a suitable air-fryer safe dish and top with the mashed sweet potato.
7. Place the dish in the preheated air fryer and cook for 20 minutes, until the top is golden brown and crisp.
8. Remove from air fryer and let it cool for 5 minutes before serving.

NUTRITION FACTS PER 100G:
Energy: 105kcal | Protein: 2.5g | Total Fat: 2.7g | Saturated Fat: 0.4g |
Carbohydrates: 17g | Sugars: 4.8g | Dietary Fibre: 2.9g

STUFFED COURGETTE BOATS

Servings: 4 | Difficulty: Easy | Temperature: 180 degrees Celsius |
Preparation Time: 20 minutes | Cooking Time: 15 minutes

INGREDIENTS:

- 4 medium-sized courgettes
- 400g minced beef
- 2 tablespoons olive oil
- 1 large onion, finely chopped
- 2 cloves of garlic, minced
- 400g tin of chopped tomatoes
- 100g cheddar cheese, grated
- 2 tablespoons fresh basil, chopped
- salt and pepper to taste

PREPARATION:

1. Halve the courgettes lengthways and scoop out the flesh, leaving a boat. Chop up the scooped-out flesh.
2. Heat the olive oil in a pan and lightly brown the beef mince.
3. Add the onion, garlic, chopped courgette flesh, and chopped tomatoes. Season with salt and pepper.
4. Simmer the mixture for 10-15 minutes until it thickens.
5. Fill the courgette boats with the mixture and sprinkle grated cheddar on top.
6. Place the stuffed courgettes in the air fryer basket.
7. Cook in the air fryer at 180 degrees Celsius for 15 minutes or until the cheese is bubbly and slightly golden.
8. Garnish with fresh basil before serving.

NUTRITION FACTS PER 100G:
Energy: 150kcal | Protein: 7.8g | Total Fat: 8.6g | Saturated Fat: 3.2g |
Carbohydrates: 5.2g | Sugars: 2.7g | Dietary Fibre: 1.0g.

VEGAN "CHICKEN" NUGGETS

Servings: 4 | Difficulty: Medium | Temperature: 180 degrees Celsius |
Preparation Time: 15 minutes | Cooking Time: 20 minutes

INGREDIENTS:

- ✪ 200g vegan chicken substitute
- ✪ 60g panko bread crumbs
- ✪ 2 tablespoons rattan flour
- ✪ 1/2 teaspoon paprika
- ✪ 1/2 teaspoon garlic granules
- ✪ 1/2 teaspoon onion powder
- ✪ 1/2 teaspoon dried thyme
- ✪ 1/2 teaspoon dried rosemary
- ✪ 2 tablespoons vegetable oil
- ✪ salt and pepper to taste

PREPARATION:

1. Cut the vegan chicken substitute into nugget-sized pieces.
2. In a bowl, mix the rattan flour, paprika, garlic granules, onion powder, dried thyme, dried rosemary, salt, and pepper.
3. Roll the vegan chicken pieces in the flour mixture until they are thoroughly coated.
4. Brush or spray the coated nuggets lightly with the vegetable oil.
5. Preheat the Air Fryer to 180 degrees Celsius.
6. Place the nuggets in the Air Fryer basket, making sure they are not touching.
7. Cook for 10 minutes, then flip the nuggets and cook for another 10 minutes or until golden and crispy.
8. Serve as desired with dipping sauces.

NUTRITION FACTS PER 100G:
Energy: 215kcal | Protein: 14g | Total Fat: 8g | Saturated Fat: 1.5g |
Carbohydrates: 18g | Sugars: 1g | Dietary Fibre: 2g

AUBERGINE PARMESAN SLICES

Servings: 4 | Difficulty: Medium | Temperature: 200 degrees Celsius |
Preparation Time: 10 minutes | Cooking Time: 10 minutes

INGREDIENTS:

- 2 medium aubergines, sliced
- 100g breadcrumbs
- 2 large free-range eggs
- 80g parmesan, finely grated
- 200g mozzarella, sliced
- 500g passata
- 1 tablespoon olive oil
- fresh basil leaves
- salt and pepper to taste

PREPARATION:

1. Preheat the Air Fryer to 200 degrees Celsius
2. Beat the eggs in a shallow bowl.
3. In a separate bowl, mix breadcrumbs, half of the Parmesan, salt, and pepper.
4. Dip each aubergine slice into the eggs, then breadcrumb mixture.
5. Arrange aubergine slices in the Air Fryer basket and cook for 5 minutes, then flip and cook for another 5 minutes.
6. In a saucepan, heat the olive oil and add passata.
7. Simmer passata for 5 minutes, then spoon over the cooked aubergine slices.
8. Top each slice with mozzarella and remaining Parmesan.
9. Return the aubergine slices to the Air Fryer and cook for 3-4 minutes until cheese is golden and bubbly.
10. Garnish with fresh basil leaves before serving.

NUTRITION FACTS PER 100G:
Energy: 133kcal | Protein: 7.9g | Total Fat: 7.0g | Saturated Fat: 2.5g |
Carbohydrates: 9.8g | Sugars: 2.6g | Dietary Fibre: 3.4g

SWEET POTATO AND BLACK BEAN BURRITOS

Servings: 4 burritos | Difficulty: Easy | Temperature: 180 Degrees Celsius |
Preparation Time: 10 minutes | Cooking Time: 25 minutes

INGREDIENTS:

- 400g sweet potatoes, peeled and cut into cubes
- 15ml olive oil
- salt and ground black pepper, to taste
- 400g black beans, rinsed and drained
- 1 chopped red onion
- 5ml minced garlic
- 1/4 teaspoon ground cumin
- 1/4 teaspoon chilli powder
- 4 large whole wheat tortillas
- 200g shredded cheddar cheese
- 50g fresh coriander, roughly chopped

PREPARATION:

1. In a large bowl, toss sweet potatoes with olive oil. Season with salt and pepper.
2. Place sweet potatoes in the air fryer basket, and cook at 180C for 15 minutes or until tender. Shake the basket halfway through cooking.
3. While the sweet potatoes are cooking, in a large pan, sauté onion and garlic until softened.
4. Add black beans, cumin, and chilli powder to the pan. Cook for an additional 2-3 minutes, stirring well.
5. Once sweet potatoes are done, combine them with the black bean mixture.
6. Warm tortillas for about 20 seconds in the microwave to make them more pliable.
7. Divide sweet potato and bean mixture equally amongst the tortillas. Add some cheese and a generous sprinkle of coriander to each. Fold ends in, and then roll up burritos.
8. Place burritos in air fryer and cook at 180C for 10 minutes or until golden brown and crispy. Be sure to flip them halfway through the cooking time.
9. Serve the burritos hot, with your favourite dips or sides.

NUTRITION FACTS PER 100G:
Energy: 180kcal | Protein: 7g | Total Fat: 6g | Saturated Fat: 3g |
Carbohydrates: 25g | Sugars: 3g | Dietary Fibre: 5g

LEEK AND POTATO SOUP CUPS

Servings: 4 | Difficulty: Easy | Temperature: 180 degrees Celsius |
Preparation Time: 20 minutes | Cooking Time: 20 minutes

INGREDIENTS:

- 300g potatoes, peeled and diced
- 200g leeks, cleaned and sliced
- 1 litre vegetable stock
- 2 tablespoons olive oil
- 1 tablespoon butter
- salt and pepper to taste
- 4 slices of crusty bread
- 2 tablespoons double cream
- fresh chives for garnish

PREPARATION:

1. Heat olive oil and butter in a large saucepan, add the sliced leeks, cook until softened.
2. Add diced potatoes, cook for another 5 minutes.
3. Pour in the vegetable stock, season with salt and pepper, simmer for 15 minutes until potatoes are tender.
4. Meanwhile, place bread slices in the air fryer, cook at 180 degrees Celsius for around 5 minutes until crispy.
5. Using a blender, blend the soup until smooth, stir in the double cream.
6. Pour the soup into the toasted bread cups, garnish with fresh chives.
7. Serve immediately.

NUTRITION FACTS PER 100G:
Energy: 75kcal | Protein: 1.8g | Total Fat: 2.5g | Saturated Fat: 0.7g |
Carbohydrates: 10.7g | Sugars: 1.1g | Dietary Fibre: 1.8g

FALAFEL AND HUMMUS WRAP

Servings: 4 | Difficulty: Medium | Temperature: 200 degrees Celsius |
Preparation Time: 20 minutes | Cooking Time: 15 minutes

INGREDIENTS:

- 400g can chickpeas, drained
- 1 small red onion, chopped
- 1 garlic clove, crushed
- 1 teaspoon ground cumin
- 1 teaspoon ground coriander (or use more cumin)
- handful parsley, chopped

- 1 teaspoon harissa paste or chilli powder
- 2 tablespoons plain flour
- 2 tablespoons sunflower or vegetable oil
- toasted pitta bread
- 200g tub tomato salsa, to serve
- For the Hummus:
- 200g can chickpeas

- 2 tablespoons lemon juice
- 2 garlic cloves, crushed
- 1 teaspoon ground cumin
- salt, to taste
- 100ml tahini paste
- 2 tablespoons water
- 2 tablespoons extra virgin olive oil
- 1 teaspoon paprika

PREPARATION:

1. Blend chickpeas, onion, garlic, cumin, coriander, parsley, and harissa for falafel mix.
2. Add flour, shape patties, and air fry at 200 degrees Celsius for 15 minutes.
3. Blend chickpeas, lemon juice, garlic, cumin, salt for hummus.
4. Mix in tahini, water, olive oil, season, and sprinkle paprika.
5. Toast pitta, fill with falafel, hummus, and salsa.
6. Enjoy your air-fried falafel with hummus!

NUTRITION FACTS PER 100G:
Energy: 220kcal | Protein: 7.5g | Total Fat: 11g | Saturated Fat: 1.6g |
Carbohydrates: 22g | Sugars: 3g | Dietary Fibre: 5g

AIR-FRIED VEGGIE PIZZA

Servings: 2 | Difficulty: Easy | Temperature: 200 degrees Celsius |
Preparation Time: 20 minutes | Cooking Time: 10 minutes

INGREDIENTS:

- 200g pre-made pizza dough
- 50ml tomato purée
- 1 tablespoon olive oil
- 1/2 teaspoon dried oregano
- 1/2 teaspoon dried basil
- 75g grated mozzarella
- 50g sliced bell peppers
- 50g sliced courgettes
- 50g sliced mushrooms
- salt and black pepper to taste

PREPARATION:

1. Roll out the pizza dough on a floured surface to a size that fits your air fryer.
2. Spread the tomato purée over the top of the dough leaving a little edge for the crust.
3. Drizzle the olive oil over the tomato purée, ensuring it spread evenly.
4. Sprinkle over the dried oregano and dried basil.
5. Add a layer of the grated mozzarella.
6. Scatter over the sliced bell peppers, courgettes, and mushrooms.
7. Season with salt and black pepper.
8. Carefully place the pizza into the air fryer.
9. Cook at 200 degrees Celsius for around 10 minutes or until the cheese is bubbling and golden.
10. Once cooked, carefully remove from the fryer and cut into slices before serving.

NUTRITION FACTS PER 100G:
Energy: 220kcal | Protein: 8g | Total Fat: 9g | Saturated Fat: 3g |
Carbohydrates: 27g | Sugars: 2g | Dietary Fibre: 2g

MUSHROOM AND STILTON WELLINGTONS

Servings: 4 | Difficulty: Medium | Temperature: 200 degrees Celsius |
Preparation Time: 25 minutes | Cooking Time: 20 minutes

INGREDIENTS:

- ✪ 4 large Portobello mushrooms
- ✪ 100g Stilton cheese
- ✪ 100g spinach leaves
- ✪ 1 small onion, finely chopped
- ✪ 2 garlic cloves, minced
- ✪ 1 tablespoon olive oil
- ✪ 1 tablespoon dried thyme
- ✪ salt and pepper to taste
- ✪ 500g puff pastry
- ✪ 1 beaten egg for glazing

PREPARATION:

1. Preheat the air fryer to 200 degrees Celsius.
2. Heat the olive oil in a frying pan and sauté the onions and garlic until translucent.
3. Add the mushrooms, spinach, thyme, salt, and pepper to the pan. Cook until the spinach wilts and the mushrooms soften.
4. Roll out puff pastry and cut into 4 rectangles.
5. Place a spoonful of the mushroom and spinach mixture on each piece of puff pastry. Crumble the Stilton cheese over the top of each.
6. Fold the pastry over the filling, press edges to seal and brush the tops with the beaten egg.
7. Place the Wellingtons in the air fryer basket, making sure they're not touching.
8. Cook in the air fryer for 20 minutes or until the Wellingtons are golden brown and crispy.
9. Serve immediately while still hot.

NUTRITION FACTS PER 100G:
Energy: 265kcal | Protein: 6.8g | Total Fat: 17.2g | Saturated Fat: 6.4g |
Carbohydrates: 24.6g | Sugars: 1.3g | Dietary Fibre: 1.5g

Chapter 6:
Sweets and Festive Treats (20 recipes)

ETON MESS BITES

Servings: 4 | Difficulty: Easy | Temperature: 180 degrees Celsius | Preparation Time: 15 minutes | Cooking Time: 10 minutes

INGREDIENTS:

- 200g of double cream
- 1 tablespoon of caster sugar
- 1 teaspoon vanilla essence
- 100g of meringue nests
- 150g of fresh strawberries
- 1 tablespoon of icing sugar
- fresh mint leaves for decoration

PREPARATION:

1. Whip the double cream with the caster sugar and vanilla essence until soft peaks form.
2. Crush the meringue nests into the whipped cream and gently fold them in.
3. Chop up half of the strawberries and fold them into the mixture.
4. Scoop spoonfuls of the mixture and place them on a tray lined with baking paper.
5. Place the tray in the air fryer and cook at 180 degrees Celsius for 10 minutes or until the bites are golden brown.
6. While the bites are cooking, create a strawberry sauce by blending the remaining strawberries with the icing sugar.
7. Once the bites are ready, take them out of the air fryer and let them cool.
8. Before serving, drizzle the strawberry sauce over the bites and garnish with fresh mint leaves.

NUTRITION FACTS PER 100G:
Energy: 250kcal | Protein: 2.5g | Total Fat: 20g | Saturated Fat: 12g | Carbohydrates: 15g | Sugars: 12g | Dietary Fibre: 0.5g

AIR-FRIED JAM DOUGHNUTS

Servings: 8 doughnuts | Difficulty: Medium | Temperature: 180 degrees Celsius | Preparation Time: 2 hours | Cooking Time: 8 minutes

INGREDIENTS:

- 250g strong white bread flour
- 25g caster sugar
- 1 teaspoon salt
- 15g fresh yeast
- 150ml milk, slightly warmed
- 1 large free-range egg
- 50g unsalted butter, softened
- 150g strawberry jam
- 50g icing sugar, for dusting
- 4 tablespoons caster sugar, for dusting
- 4 tablespoons water

PREPARATION:

1. Start by combining the flour, sugar, and salt in a large mixing bowl.
2. Dissolve the yeast in the warm milk, then add to the dry ingredients along with the egg.
3. Use your hands to combine the ingredients until a sticky dough forms.
4. Add the softened butter, then knead the dough until it becomes smooth and elastic.
5. Allow the dough to rest in a warm area until it doubles in size, usually about an hour.
6. Once the dough has risen, divide it into 8 equal pieces.
7. Roll each piece into a ball, then place onto a lined baking tray.
8. Let the dough balls prove for an additional hour, they should double in size again.
9. Preheat the air fryer to 180 degrees Celsius.
10. Cook the doughnuts for about 4 minutes each side or until they are golden brown.
11. Allow to cool slightly, then inject each doughnut with approximately 1 tablespoon of strawberry jam.
12. In a pan, mix the caster sugar and water, bring to boil and cook until the mixture thickens a little to make simple syrup.
13. Brush each doughnut with the simple syrup, and a dusting of icing sugar.
14. Serve while the doughnuts are still warm.

NUTRITION FACTS PER 100G:
Energy: 276kcal | Protein: 7.6g | Total Fat: 6.2g | Saturated Fat: 2.8g | Carbohydrates: 46.9g | Sugars: 15.2g | Dietary Fibre: 1.7g

LEMON DRIZZLE CAKE SQUARES

Servings: 16 squares | Difficulty: Easy | Temperature: 160 degrees Celsius | Preparation Time: 15 minutes | Cooking Time: 25 minutes

INGREDIENTS:

- ✪ 200g self-raising flour
- ✪ 200g caster sugar
- ✪ 200g unsalted butter, at room temperature
- ✪ 4 large eggs
- ✪ zest of 2 lemons
- ✪ 2 tablespoons lemon juice
- ✪ 150g icing sugar
- ✪ 2 tablespoons warm water

PREPARATION:

1. In a large mixing bowl, beat together the caster sugar and butter until light and fluffy.
2. Beat the eggs in a separate bowl, then add them to the sugar and butter mixture, mixing well.
3. Add the lemon zest and 1 tablespoon lemon juice to the bowl and mix until combined.
4. Sift the flour into the mixture and mix well.
5. Spoon the mixture into a silicone square cake mould that will fit into your air fryer basket. Smooth the top with a palette knife.
6. Preheat the air fryer to 160 degrees Celsius.
7. Cook the cake in the air fryer for 25 minutes, or until a skewer inserted into the centre comes out clean.
8. Let the cake cool for 10 minutes in the mould, then remove and place on a cooling rack.
9. While the cake is cooling, prepare the icing by combining the icing sugar, remaining lemon juice and warm water. Stir until it has a pouring consistency.
10. Once the cake has cooled completely, drizzle the icing over the squares.
11. Allow the icing to set before serving.

NUTRITION FACTS PER 100G:
Energy: 406kcal | Protein: 5.6g | Total Fat: 21g | Saturated Fat: 13g | Carbohydrates: 50g | Sugars: 35g | Dietary Fibre: 1g

CHOCOLATE FONDUE CUPS

Servings: 4 | Difficulty: Easy | Temperature: 175 degrees Celsius |
Preparation Time: 5 minutes | Cooking Time: 10 minutes

INGREDIENTS:

- 200g of dark chocolate
- 50ml of double cream
- 2 tablespoons of unsalted butter
- 8 ready-made pastry dough cups
- fresh fruits of your choice for serving (e.g. strawberries, bananas, grapes)

PREPARATION:

1. Preheat your air fryer at 175 degrees Celsius.
2. In a microwave-safe bowl, melt chocolate, double cream, and unsalted butter for 1 minute, stirring every 20 seconds to avoid burning the mixture.
3. Pour the fondue mixture into the dough cups, not exceeding three-quarters full.
4. Carefully place the cups in the preheated air fryer and set the timer for 10 minutes, or until the chocolate becomes gooey.
5. Let the cups cool for a few minutes after frying, then serve alongside your preferred fresh fruits.
6. Berries such as strawberries are a nice counterpoint to the rich chocolate. Use sticks or skewers to dip the fruit into the hot chocolate.

NUTRITION FACTS PER 100G:
Energy: 410kcal | Protein: 5g | Total Fat: 27g | Saturated Fat: 16g |
Carbohydrates: 35g | Sugars: 20g | Dietary Fibre: 3.2g

MINI CHRISTMAS PUDDINGS

Servings: 6 | Difficulty: Medium | Temperature: 180 degrees Celsius |
Preparation Time: 30 minutes | Cooking Time: 15 minutes

INGREDIENTS:

- 800g mixed dried fruit (raisins, currants, sultanas, dried cherries)
- 125ml brandy
- zest and juice of 1 orange
- 175g light muscovado sugar
- 85g plain flour
- 100g breadcrumbs from a day-old loaf
- 1 tablespoon spice mix nutmeg, cinnamon, allspice
- 2 large eggs
- 50g unsalted butter, melted
- additional: miniature aluminium pudding moulds

PREPARATION:

1. Put the mixed dried fruit with the brandy, zest and juice of the orange in a large bowl. Leave it overnight to soak.
2. In a different bowl, combine the sugar, flour, breadcrumbs and spice mix.
3. Beat the eggs and add to your dry ingredients, followed by the melted butter. Mix thoroughly.
4. Add the soaked fruit into your pudding mixture and stir well to combine.
5. Grease the aluminium pudding moulds and fill each one with the mixture.
6. Place the moulds in the air fryer basket, ensuring there is enough space between each.
7. Cook in the preheated air fryer at 180 degrees Celsius for 15 minutes, or until risen and firm to the touch.
8. Allow to cool and then remove from the moulds.

NUTRITION FACTS PER 100G:
Energy: 320kcal | Protein: 3.5g | Total Fat: 5.2g | Saturated Fat: 3.1g |
Carbohydrates: 65.6g | Sugars: 48.5g | Dietary Fibre: 4.9g

AIR-FRIED WELSH CAKES

Servings: 8 cakes | Difficulty: Medium | Temperature: 180 degrees Celsius | Preparation Time: 20 minutes | Cooking Time: 10 minutes

INGREDIENTS:

- 225g self-raising flour
- 1 teaspoon mixed spice
- 75g caster sugar
- 100g unsalted butter
- 75g currants
- 1 medium egg
- 2 tablespoons milk
- a little extra sugar for sprinkling

PREPARATION:

1. In a large bowl, combine the self-raising flour and mixed spice.
2. Add the caster sugar, followed by the butter, and rub together to a breadcrumb consistency.
3. Stir in the currants.
4. Beat the egg in a separate bowl, then add to the mixture along with the milk, and stir until you have soft dough.
5. On a floured surface, roll out the dough to about 1cm thickness, and cut into rounds with a 6cm cutter.
6. Preheat the air fryer to 180 degrees Celsius.
7. Arrange the cakes spaced apart in the air fryer basket.
8. Cook for 5 minutes, then turn them over and cook for a further 5 minutes.
9. Remove from the air fryer and sprinkle with a little extra sugar while still warm.
10. Allow them to cool on a wire rack before serving.

NUTRITION FACTS PER 100G:
Energy: 370kcal | Protein: 5.5g | Total Fat: 13.5g | Saturated Fat: 8g | Carbohydrates: 58g | Sugars: 16g | Dietary Fibre: 2g

STICKY TOFFEE PUDDING BITES

Servings: 4 | Difficulty: Moderate | Temperature: 180 Degrees Celsius |
Preparation Time: 20 minutes | Cooking Time: 10 minutes

INGREDIENTS:

- 150g chopped dates
- 200ml boiling water
- 1 teaspoon bicarbonate of soda
- 50g butter, at room temperature
- 60g caster sugar
- 60g dark brown sugar
- 2 eggs
- 150g self-raising flour
- 1 teaspoon vanilla extract
- 2 tablespoons black treacle
- for the sticky toffee sauce:
- 100g butter
- 200g dark brown sugar
- 200ml double cream

PREPARATION:

1. Soak the chopped dates in the boiling water along with the bicarbonate of soda and set aside for 10 minutes.
2. In a separate bowl, cream the butter and sugars together until light and fluffy.
3. Beat in the eggs, one at a time, until well combined.
4. Gradually add the flour, mixing well after each addition.
5. Stir in the soaked date mixture, vanilla extract and black treacle.
6. Pour the mixture into a greased air fryer-safe cake tin.
7. Cook in the air fryer at 180 degrees Celsius for 10 minutes or until a toothpick comes out clean.
8. Meanwhile, make the sauce by melting the butter, sugar and cream in a saucepan over medium heat.
9. Pour the sauce over the cooked pudding bites and serve warm.

NUTRITION FACTS PER 100G:
Energy: 340kcal | Protein: 4g | Total Fat: 14g | Saturated Fat: 8g |
Carbohydrates: 50g | Sugars: 35g | Dietary Fibre: 1g

ECCLES CAKE PARCELS

Servings: 8 | Difficulty: Medium | Temperature: 160 degrees Celsius | Preparation Time: 40 minutes | Cooking Time: 15 minutes

INGREDIENTS:

- ✪ 200g puff pastry
- ✪ 75g currants
- ✪ 50g unsalted butter
- ✪ 50g dark brown sugar

- ✪ 1/2 teaspoon ground cinnamon
- ✪ 1/2 teaspoon mixed spices
- ✪ zest of one lemon
- ✪ a pinch of salt

- ✪ 2 tablespoons water
- ✪ 1 egg (for egg wash)
- ✪ 2 tablespoons demerara sugar

PREPARATION:

1. Roll out the puff pastry about 3mm thickness and cut into 8, 10cm squares. Set aside.
2. Combine currants, unsalted butter, dark brown sugar, ground cinnamon, mixed spices, lemon zest, and a pinch of salt in a pan, stir on medium heat until the butter has melted.
3. Add water and simmer until the mixture comes together, then set aside to cool.
4. Once cooled, spoon the mixture onto the centre of each cut-out puff pastry square.
5. Fold corners of the pastry to the centre to create a parcel, pressing it gently to seal.
6. Preheat the air fryer to 160 degrees Celsius and gently brush each parcel with the whisked egg, then sprinkle with demerara sugar.
7. Air fry the parcels for 15 minutes or until golden brown.
8. Let cool for a few minutes in the basket before serving on a cooling rack.

> **NUTRITION FACTS PER 100G:**
> Energy: 380kcal | Protein: 5.2g | Total Fat: 21.7g | Saturated Fat: 10.1g | Carbohydrates: 41.1g | Sugars: 16.9g | Dietary Fibre: 1.4g

SPOTTED DICK SLICES

Servings: 6 | Difficulty: Medium | Temperature: 180 degrees Celsius |
Preparation Time: 20 minutes | Cooking Time: 25 minutes

INGREDIENTS:

- 150g self-raising flour
- 70g shredded suet
- 50g caster sugar
- 75g currants
- zest of 1 lemon
- 2 tablespoons brown sugar
- 1 tablespoon baking powder
- 150ml milk
- a pinch of salt
- cooking spray
- serving suggestion: custard, for serving

PREPARATION:

1. In a mixing bowl, combine the self-raising flour, shredded suet, baking powder, caster sugar, currants, salt, and lemon zest.
2. Gradually stir in the milk until the mixture forms a wet dough.
3. Preheat your Air Fryer to 180 degrees Celsius.
4. Lightly grease a baking tin with cooking spray. Pour in the dough mix and smooth the top.
5. Sprinkle the brown sugar evenly over the mix.
6. Carefully place the tin into the Air Fryer and cook for approximately 25 minutes, or until a skewer comes out clean when inserted into the middle.
7. Once cooked, remove spotted dick from Air Fryer and let cool.
8. After cooling, slice your spotted dick into 6 equal portions.
9. Serve warm with a dollop of custard.

NUTRITION FACTS PER 100G:
Energy: 295kcal | Protein: 4g | Total Fat: 10g | Saturated Fat: 4g |
Carbohydrates: 47g | Sugars: 18g | Dietary Fibre: 1g

MINI BAKEWELL TARTS

Servings: 12 | Difficulty: Medium | Temperature: 180 degrees Celsius |
Preparation Time: 25 minutes | Cooking Time: 12 minutes

INGREDIENTS:

- 375g ready-rolled shortcrust pastry
- 135g raspberry jam
- 150g ground almonds
- 150g caster sugar
- 150g melted unsalted butter
- 3 free-range eggs
- 1 teaspoon almond extract
- 100g icing sugar
- 2 tablespoons water
- 12 glace cherries

PREPARATION:

1. Roll out the pastry and cut 12 discs using a pastry cutter.
2. Place each disc in the compartments of a muffin tin.
3. Spoon 1 tablespoon of raspberry jam into the base of each pastry case.
4. In a bowl, mix together the ground almonds, caster sugar, butter, eggs, and almond extract until well combined.
5. Spoon the mixture into the pastry cases on top of the jam.
6. Place the muffin tin in the air fryer and cook at 180 degrees Celsius for 12 minutes.
7. Allow the tarts to cool in the tin for 10 minutes, then transfer to a wire rack to cool completely.
8. For the icing, mix together the icing sugar and water to create a smooth paste. Spoon over the top of each tart.
9. Top each tart with a glace cherry and serve.

NUTRITION FACTS PER 100G:
Energy: 300kcal | Protein: 4.5g | Total Fat: 20g | Saturated Fat: 7.8g |
Carbohydrates: 27g | Sugars: 16g | Dietary Fibre: 1.8g

CHOCOLATE ECLAIRS

Servings: 12 eclairs | Difficulty: Medium | Temperature: 180 degrees Celsius | Preparation Time: 35 minutes | Cooking Time: 15 minutes

INGREDIENTS:

- ✪ 225ml water
- ✪ 85g unsalted butter
- ✪ 1/4 teaspoon salt
- ✪ 130g plain flour
- ✪ 4 large eggs

- ✪ 175g dark chocolate
- ✪ 250ml double cream
- ✪ 100g granulated sugar
- ✪ 2 tablespoons cornflour
- ✪ 4 egg yolks

- ✪ 2 teaspoons pure vanilla extract
- ✪ 2 tablespoons icing sugar

PREPARATION:

1. Preheat the air fryer to 180 degrees Celsius.
2. In a saucepan, combine the water, butter, and salt and heat until the butter melts.
3. Add the flour into the mixture, mixing vigorously until a dough forms.
4. Allow the dough to cool, then incorporate one egg at a time.
5. Shape the dough into elongated balls and place in the air fryer.
6. Cook for 15 minutes or until golden-brown.
7. Allow to cool, then slice each in half.
8. In a pan, heat the double cream, granulated sugar, and cornflour stirring continuously until it begins to thicken.
9. Lower the heat and add the egg yolks and vanilla extract, stirring until it thickens into custard.
10. Fill the eclairs with the custard.
11. Melt the chocolate and drizzle over the filled eclairs.
12. Dust with icing sugar before serving.

NUTRITION FACTS PER 100G:
Energy: 297kcal | Protein: 5.5g | Total Fat: 21g | Saturated Fat: 12g | Carbohydrates: 23g | Sugars: 15g | Dietary Fibre: 1.5g

TREACLE TART CUPS

Servings: 4 | Difficulty: Medium | Temperature: 180 degrees Celsius |
Preparation Time: 20 minutes | Cooking Time: 15 minutes

INGREDIENTS:

- 200g shortcrust pastry
- 200g golden syrup
- 100ml double cream
- 2 medium eggs
- 75g fresh breadcrumbs
- 1 tablespoon lemon juice
- 1 tablespoon grated lemon zest

PREPARATION:

1. Roll out the pastry until it is about 3mm thick.
2. Cut out circles from the pastry which will fit into your air fryer cup fitting.
3. Press each circle into a cup mould, prick the base with a fork, and refrigerate for 10 minutes.
4. Preheat air fryer to 180 degrees Celsius.
5. In a pan, gently heat the golden syrup and double cream together until combined.
6. Break the eggs into the syrup mixture, followed by the breadcrumbs, lemon juice, and lemon zest.
7. Stir briskly until all the ingredients are thoroughly mixed.
8. Take your tart cups out of the fridge and fill with the syrup mixture.
9. Place the tart cups inside the air fryer basket.
10. Cook for 15 minutes or until the pastry is golden and the filling has set.
11. Once done, take the tart cups out carefully and let them cool down before serving.

NUTRITION FACTS PER 100G:
Energy: 325kcal | Protein: 3.5g | Total Fat: 14g | Saturated Fat: 7g |
Carbohydrates: 44g | Sugars: 24g | Dietary Fibre: 1g

AIR-FRIED SCONES WITH CLOTTED CREAM

Servings: 8 scones | Difficulty: Medium | Temperature: 180 degrees Celsius |
Preparation Time: 20 minutes | Cooking Time: 12 minutes

INGREDIENTS:

- 225g self-raising flour
- 1/2 teaspoon baking powder
- 50g unsalted butter
- 25g caster sugar
- 100ml milk
- 1 teaspoon pure vanilla extract
- 1 egg, beaten
- 150g clotted cream
- 50g strawberry jam

PREPARATION:

1. Combine the self-raising flour and baking powder in a large bowl.
2. Add the unsalted butter to the bowl and rub it into the flour until it resembles fine breadcrumbs.
3. Stir in the caster sugar.
4. Warm the milk in the microwave until hot but not boiling, then add vanilla extract.
5. Make a well in the flour mixture, pour in the warm milk, and mix until you have a soft dough.
6. Turn the dough out onto a lightly floured surface and knead briefly.
7. Press the dough out to a 2cm thick round, then use a round biscuit cutter to cut out scones.
8. Brush the tops with the beaten egg.
9. Preheat the air fryer to 180 degrees Celsius.
10. Arrange the scones in the fryer basket, making sure they are not touching.
11. Cook for 12 minutes, until golden brown.
12. Serve the scones warm with generous dollops of clotted cream and strawberry jam.

NUTRITION FACTS PER 100G:
Energy: 210kcal | Protein: 2.9g | Total Fat: 9.5g | Saturated Fat: 5.2g |
Carbohydrates: 27.7g | Sugars: 9.1g | Dietary Fibre: 0.7g

APPLE AND BLACKBERRY CRUMBLE BITES

Servings: 6 | Difficulty: Medium | Temperature: 180 degrees Celsius |
Preparation Time: 15 minutes | Cooking Time: 15 minutes

INGREDIENTS:

- ✪ 3 medium apples, peeled and cubed
- ✪ 150g blackberries
- ✪ 100g caster sugar

- ✪ 1 tablespoon lemon juice
- ✪ 100g plain flour
- ✪ 75g butter, chilled and diced

- ✪ 50g rolled oats
- ✪ 2 tablespoons honey

PREPARATION:

1. In a bowl, mix apples, blackberries, 50g of the sugar, and lemon juice. Set aside for 10 minutes to marinate.
2. Make the crumble by placing flour and remaining 50g sugar in a separate bowl, add chilled diced butter and rub together until the mixture resembles breadcrumbs.
3. Stir in the rolled oats into the crumble mixture.
4. Divide the apple and blackberry mixture among six individual silicon moulds.
5. Top the fruit mixture in each mould with the crumble mixture.
6. Lightly drizzle each crumble with honey.
7. Pop the moulds into the air fryer basket. Set the air fryer to 180 degrees Celsius and bake for 15 minutes or until the crumble topping is golden and crisp.
8. Allow to cool slightly, before carefully turning out the crumble bites. Serve warm.

NUTRITION FACTS PER 100G:
Energy: 170kcal | Protein: 2.1g | Total Fat: 5.9g | Saturated Fat: 3.6g |
Carbohydrates: 28.2g | Sugars: 18.3g | Dietary Fibre: 2.5g

MINCE PIE CUPS

Servings: 6 | Difficulty: Medium | Temperature: 180 degrees Celsius |
Preparation Time: 20 minutes | Cooking Time: 15 minutes

INGREDIENTS:

- ✪ 250g plain flour
- ✪ 125g unsalted butter, chilled and diced
- ✪ 2-3 tablespoons cold water
- ✪ 300g mincemeat (fruit variety)
- ✪ icing sugar for dusting

PREPARATION:

1. In a large bowl, mix the flour and butter until they resemble breadcrumbs.
2. Slowly add water, mixing until the dough binds together.
3. Once dough is formed, wrap it in cling film and chill for 10-15 minutes.
4. While dough is chilling, place mincemeat into a bowl and stir, breaking up any large pieces.
5. After dough is chilled, roll it out thinly and cut out 12 discs using a round cutter.
6. Press the discs into the cups of a muffin tin.
7. Spoon the mincemeat into the cups, spreading evenly.
8. Take remaining dough, roll out again and cut out 6 smaller discs. Place on top of each filled cup, pressing edges together.
9. Place muffin tin in preheated air fryer at 180 degrees Celsius and bake for 15 minutes or until pie cups are golden brown.
10. Allow to cool slightly, then remove from muffin tin. Dust with icing sugar and serve.

NUTRITION FACTS PER 100G:
Energy: 280kcal | Protein: 3.1g | Total Fat: 13.2g | Saturated Fat: 7.9g |
Carbohydrates: 33.6g | Sugars: 13.8g | Dietary Fibre: 1.2g

RASPBERRY AND WHITE CHOCOLATE MUFFINS

Servings: 12 muffins | Difficulty: Easy | Temperature: 160 degrees Celsius |
Preparation Time: 15 minutes | Cooking Time: 15 minutes

INGREDIENTS:

- 250g self-raising flour
- 125g caster sugar
- 60g unsalted butter, melted
- 2 large eggs
- 125ml milk
- 1 teaspoon pure vanilla extract
- 100g white chocolate chips
- 100g fresh raspberries
- a pinch of salt
- 12 paper muffin cases

PREPARATION:

1. Combine the self-raising flour, caster sugar, and pinch of salt in a large bowl.
2. In a separate bowl, whisk together the melted butter, eggs, milk, and vanilla extract.
3. Gradually add the wet ingredients to the dry ingredients, stirring just until combined.
4. Fold in the white chocolate chips and fresh raspberries, taking care not to over mix.
5. Line the air fryer basket with the paper muffin cases and evenly divide the batter among them.
6. Set the air fryer to 160 degrees Celsius and bake for 15 minutes, or until a toothpick inserted into the centre of a muffin comes out clean.
7. Let muffins cool in the air fryer for a few minutes, then transfer to a wire rack to cool completely.

NUTRITION FACTS PER 100G:
Energy: 390kcal | Protein: 6g | Total Fat: 15g | Saturated Fat: 8g |
Carbohydrates: 57g | Sugars: 28g | Dietary Fibre: 1g

BANOFFEE PIE BITES

Servings: 12 | Difficulty: Medium | Temperature: 200 degrees Celsius |
Preparation Time: 30 minutes | Cooking Time: 15 minutes

INGREDIENTS:

- 200g digestive biscuits
- 70g unsalted butter, melted
- 1 can (397g) Dulce de Leche
- 3 small bananas
- 300ml double cream
- 2 tablespoons caster sugar
- 1 chocolate bar (for garnishing)

PREPARATION:

1. Crush the digestive biscuits in a food processor until they turn into fine crumbs.
2. Mix the biscuit crumbs with the melted butter, then spoon them into an air fryer friendly dish.
3. Press the crumbs down to form a firm base, then place the dish into the fridge for about 20 minutes to set.
4. Once the base is set, spread the Dulce de Leche on top of it.
5. Slice the bananas and arrange them on top of the Dulce de Leche.
6. In a mixing bowl, whip the double cream and caster sugar until soft peaks form.
7. Gently spread the whipped cream over the banana slices.
8. Grate the chocolate bar on top of the whipped cream for garnishing.
9. Place the dish in the pre-heated air fryer, and cook for 15 minutes at 200 degrees Celsius.
10. Allow to cool before cutting into bite-sized pieces and serving.

NUTRITION FACTS PER 100G:
Energy: 350kcal | Protein: 3g | Total Fat: 23g | Saturated Fat: 14g |
Carbohydrates: 32g | Sugars: 20g | Dietary Fibre: 1.3g

CHOCOLATE AND ORANGE BREAD AND BUTTER PUDDING

Servings: 6 | Difficulty: Medium | Temperature: 180 degrees Celsius |
Preparation Time: 20 minutes | Cooking Time: 25 minutes

INGREDIENTS:

- 8 slices thick bread
- 100g dark chocolate
- zest of 1 large orange
- 50g unsalted butter, plus extra for greasing
- 2 large eggs
- 350ml whole milk
- 50ml double cream
- 1 teaspoon pure vanilla extract
- 50g granulated sugar

PREPARATION:

1. Tear up the bread into chunks and place them in a bowl.
2. Melt the chocolate and butter in a pan over low heat, then pour over the bread chunks and stir to combine.
3. Add in the orange zest and mix well. Grease your air fryer basket with butter.
4. In a separate bowl, whisk together the eggs, milk, double cream, vanilla extract and sugar.
5. Pour the egg mixture over the bread chunks and push down with a spoon to ensure all bread is soaked.
6. Spoon the bread mixture into the air fryer basket and cook at 180 degrees Celsius for 25 minutes, or until the pudding is set and golden on top.
7. Let cool slightly before serving - enjoy hot or cold.

NUTRITION FACTS PER 100G:
Energy: 247kcal | Protein: 5.4g | Total Fat: 10g | Saturated Fat: 5g |
Carbohydrates: 31g | Sugars: 16g | Dietary Fibre: 1.5g

AIR-FRIED HOT CROSS BUNS

Servings: 12 buns | Difficulty: Medium | Temperature: 160 degrees Celsius |
Preparation Time: 2 hours | Cooking Time: 8 minutes

INGREDIENTS:

- 500g strong white bread flour
- 75g caster sugar
- 1 tablespoon mixed spice powder
- 1 tablespoon ground cinnamon
- 10g salt
- 10g instant yeast
- 40g softened unsalted butter
- 2 medium eggs
- 120ml warm milk
- 120ml warm water
- 150g mixed dried fruit
- for the cross: 75g plain flour, 75ml water
- for the glaze: 2 tablespoons golden syrup

PREPARATION:

1. First, combine bread flour, caster sugar, mixed spice, cinnamon, salt, and yeast in a large bowl.
2. Add the softened butter, eggs, warm milk, and water to the mixture.
3. Stir until you have a soft, but not sloppy, dough.
4. Now, mix the dried fruit into the dough.
5. Turn the dough out onto a lightly-floured surface and knead by hand for 10 minutes, or until it's smooth and stretchy.
6. Place your dough in a lightly-oiled bowl, cover with a kitchen towel, and leave it to rise for about an hour or until doubled in size.
7. Once risen, turn your dough out onto a floured surface again, divide it into 12 even pieces, and shape each into a round bun.
8. Place your buns in the air fryer basket, allowing some space between them, and prove for another hour until they are touching.
9. For the cross on the buns, mix the plain flour and water together until smooth. Pipe crosses on the top of each bun.
10. Preheat your air fryer to 160 degrees Celsius and cook the buns for 8-10 minutes, or until golden brown.
11. For the glaze, gently heat the golden syrup in a small saucepan or in the microwave, then brush it over the top of the warm buns.
12. Remove your air fried hot cross buns and allow them to cool before serving.

> **NUTRITION FACTS PER 100G:**
> Energy: 297kcal | Protein: 8g | Total Fat: 3.5g | Saturated Fat: 1.8g |
> Carbohydrates: 56g | Sugars: 14g | Dietary Fibre: 2.5g

BLACK FOREST GATEAU CUPS

Servings: 4 | Difficulty: Easy | Temperature: 160 degrees Celsius |
Preparation Time: 15 minutes | Cooking Time: 15 minutes

INGREDIENTS:

- 200g digestive biscuits
- 100g unsalted butter, melted
- 400g cherry pie filling
- 200g dark chocolate, melted
- 300ml double cream
- 2 tablespoons icing sugar
- 1 tablespoon vanilla extract
- 4 fresh cherries, for topping

PREPARATION:

1. Crush the Digestive biscuits into fine crumbs.
2. Mix in the melted butter and press into the base of four ramekins.
3. Spoon the cherry pie filling evenly over the biscuit base.
4. Pour melted dark chocolate over the cherry filling, ensuring it's evenly spread.
5. Place ramekins in the air fryer and cook at 160 degrees Celsius for 10 minutes.
6. While gateau is cooling, whisk together double cream, icing sugar and vanilla extract until soft peaks form.
7. Pipe or dollop the whipped cream onto each of the cooled gateau.
8. Top each one with a fresh cherry before serving.

NUTRITION FACTS PER 100G:
Energy: 243kcal | Protein: 2.9g | Total Fat: 14.2g | Saturated Fat: 7.5g |
Carbohydrates: 26.6g | Sugars: 16.8g | Dietary Fibre: 1.6g

Disclaimer

The recipes provided in „The XXL Air Fryer Cookbook UK" are intended for informational purposes only. While every effort has been made to ensure the accuracy and safety of the recipes, we cannot guarantee individual results or the appropriateness of ingredients for specific dietary needs or restrictions.

Readers are advised to use their discretion and consult with a qualified healthcare professional or nutritionist regarding any dietary concerns or allergies. It is the responsibility of the reader to carefully review the ingredients and cooking instructions, and to make any necessary adjustments based on personal preferences or dietary requirements.

Furthermore, the authors and publishers of this cookbook disclaim any liability for any loss, damage, or injury caused by the use or misuse of the information provided within. Cooking with air fryers involves the use of heat and kitchen appliances, and proper safety precautions should always be followed.

By using this cookbook, readers acknowledge and accept the inherent risks associated with cooking and agree to indemnify the authors and publishers from any claims arising from the use of the recipes or information contained herein.

We hope you enjoy exploring the delicious recipes in this cookbook and encourage you to cook with confidence and creativity. Happy air frying!

EXCLUSIVE BONUS

40 Weight Loss Recipes

&

14 Days Meal Plan

Scan the QR-Code and receive
the FREE download: